WILL IT BE
ON THE EXAM?

21 Stories About Unforgettable Students

MELVIN H. GREEN, PHD

ISBN: 1470048817
ISBN 13: 9781470048815

Library of Congress Control Number: 2012903239
CreateSpace, North Charleston, SC

MEET PROFESSOR GREEN'S UNFORGETTABLE STUDENTS

With fifty years of university teaching behind him, during which he taught more than 20,000 students, Professor Melvin Green shares his insights and experiences about a diverse set of unforgettable students. You will laugh and cry as you learn about them through the keen eye and sharp wit of this highly awarded and much loved professor. Don't be surprised when you see yourself in there at times.

Mel Green was the first in his family to attend college, majoring in Chemistry at the U. of Pittsburgh. He received a Ph.D. in Biochemistry from the U. of Illinois in 1962, and after a year of post-doctoral research at Cal Tech, took a position as an Assistant Professor of Biology at the recently founded U. of California, San Diego. His research on the mechanism of gene regulation led to an award as Scholar in Cancer Research from the American Cancer Society and a sabbatical year in London at the Imperial Cancer Research Fund from 1970-71.

Returning to UCSD, Dr. Green climbed the academic ranks to Professor on the basis of his research and teaching accomplishments. He created many new courses, including The Molecular Basis of Disease, Virology, The Biology of Cancer, and Classic Experiments in Modern Biology. The latter was based on a book he wrote with that title. Dr. Green's close interactions with many students was also greatly enhanced by his serving as director of the Academic Enrichment Programs and of the Hughes Scholars Program for a total of eight years. To maintain contact with undergraduates after his retirement, Dr. Green recently founded the Emeritus Mentor Program, which serves first generation college students at UCSD.

Readers' Comments

As a student, I have a great interest in reading what life is like from the Professor's point of view, and I am sure other students, especially college students, share the same interest. What I find most enjoyable about your writing is how completely honest and open you are. Your insights are always profound and meaningful, your humor is genuine, and your composure is modest and inviting. Your stories really show your compassionate, human side; a side which is often left mysterious and undiscovered by students who interact with professors on a daily basis.

Joseph Lee,
UCSD undergraduate

I found it interesting that you interspersed stories from the 60s with those from the 90s or 2000s. An example being Shaken Dreams at the beginning of your career in comparison with **Sexism**, where the boyfriend breaks up by email. It helped me realize that although some of these may be forty years old, they are just as relevant today as they were then.

Ross Castillo,
UCSD undergraduate

I must say I really, really liked this! It's very interesting to see the world of the classroom through the eyes of the professor. One always sees it from the other side.

Iris Monica Vargas,
M.S. in Physics, M.S. in Science Writing

I am very impressed with your ability to convey ideas and emotions with very few words. You have a talent that ranges far beyond Biology. All I can say is that you can "scribble" — and that's high praise indeed in the world of journalism and literature.

Peter Clark,
PhD in History, sports journalist and teacher

It is sincere, honest, enlightening, and engaging. I loved all the little anecdotes and stories about students you have interacted with.

Suzan Cioffi, Director,
UCSD Retirement Resource Center

I was totally charmed by your stories. So wonderfully human (like some of your teaching methods). The read is spiritually elevating and the good kind of funny, sometimes even a little slap-stick; and that's difficult to do in prose. Technically, your use of pace and time is wonderful. Very conscious of possible impatience of your reader, you leave them wanting more. If there is an inverse of professorial garrulousness, you found it. Of course, the best of the book is your voice. A sharp but gentle pixie.

This would make a nice gift for incoming students.

With the properly provocative cover it could be a best seller in university book stores for sure.

Dr. Arnold Mandell
Professor Emeritus and founder of Psychiatry Dept., UCSD

PROLOGUE

I get to my class a few minutes before the hour. I want to be early so I can meet the TAs before starting to lecture. The room fills up with students, more than 300 of them, all talking to someone about what a great summer they had, where they went, what they did in all parts of the world, how they got into a lab and did some research that was "sooo exciting." They find a seat and keep on talking past the start of the hour when I'm supposed to begin lecturing about the wonders of Biology, the Science of Life, but not their life. Right now, their life is more important to them, and they keep on talking while I receive hugs and welcome backs from the TAs who know me from last year, and meet those who are new this year. Now all the seats are taken, and they keep coming in, sitting on the stairs in the aisles, still chattering away about their own lives, which are far more important than the Science of Life. I check my watch and it's ten past the hour and I haven't said a word yet to the class. I just stand there watching them, jealous of their enthusiasm and their youth, and all that goes and comes with it. Finally they see me and realize they are in their next class and the Professor wants to begin his lecture, and the noise gradually dies down from a roar to a background hum, and I say my first words to my new class. "The subject of today's lecture is 'What Is Living?' Does anyone have an answer to this simple question?" The silence of the lambs is stunning. Not one hand is raised. They expect to wait me out; then I will answer my own simple question, and they get out their notebooks, ready to write every word the Professor says so they can get an A on his exams and get on the Dean's list and graduate with high honors and get into Medical School or Graduate School and get a great job like the Professor has. Only I don't answer my own question. I can wait it out, too. I look around the first few rows at the faces, knowing that a few of them will actually become known to me. They will come to see me during an office hour, or for a coffee or lunch if brave enough, or maybe even a game of tennis, telling me their problems with school or family or a friend, and their goals in life, almost never asking anything about me. My life is set, everything is done, and it's of no use to them. So I listen and listen and throw in a word here and there, and they like me, and that makes me feel happy and important. Being a professor is such a great ego trip.

I know I help some of them in some small way. From what they tell me, not many other professors even listen to them. But I also know my students help me a lot along this journey of Life, so I want to share some stories about them in the hope that they will help you, too. Some of these stories are about specific students, others pertain more to classroom events. They are not arranged in any particular chronological order. The names have been changed to protect both the innocent and the guilty. I assure the reader that to the best of my memory, all these stories are accurate even if some seem unbelievable.

Contents

1.

TENNIS ANYONE?

"I know there are a lot of scientists in this program and this will be hard for you, but throughout this weekend I want you to stop thinking and start feeling. Every time you say 'I think,' stop and say 'I feel.'"

Those were the words of the famous psychologist, Dr. Carl Rogers, at the start of a program I attended soon after my arrival in La Jolla. Dr. Rogers had recently created the Center for Studies of the Person in La Jolla, and my attendance at one of his weekend programs provided a clear insight into his philosophy. Of special interest to me as a young professor were his ideas about education. We must learn to feel, not merely think, that all people, including students and teachers, are equal. Then we can do better at treating everyone as equals.

A few weeks after attending Dr. Rogers' program, I visited him at his Center. I was greatly influenced by his thoughts on education and came away with an important gift... his book, "Freedom to Learn." I came to realize that in the realm of education, the teacher acts as lord and master while the student is kept in a state of total subjugation. All of the rules are set by the teacher with no input from the student. The classroom is arranged with the teacher in front, often on a platform and behind a podium, while the students are seated in rows facing the teacher. Coincidentally, a popular book of that period was entitled "A Nation of Sheep." It emphasizes the point that we are taught to follow, not to lead. Dr. Rogers prefers a circular orientation in the classroom, with the teacher being one equal member of the circle. As he put it, we can all learn from one another. The teacher should facilitate that learning.

From my earliest days as a teacher at UCSD, I thought about Carl Rogers' views on education. With graduate student class sizes of less than 20, it was not so difficult to promote student participation. I selected the research papers for the entire class to read, and the group of students assigned to that paper played the roles of the authors. One would present the summary and introduction, another the methods, another the results, and one would present the discussion of the paper. The other students would be free to comment and ask questions at any time. Harvey Hershman, a student in my very first class and now a professor at UCLA, tells his students how he played the role of Daisy Dussoix in a paper that opened the door to genetic engineering and led to a Nobel prize for the senior author, Werner Arber. The fact that Harvey still remembers the name of the author he role-played more than 40 years later is indicative of the impact this method of teaching has on students. Professor Hershman still employs the same successful method of teaching in his graduate courses.

Introducing equality into a classroom with 300 under-graduate students is a far more difficult task than in a small graduate course. There is a huge barrier between professors and undergraduate students in the university, much greater than that in junior and senior high school. Most professors have a keen ability to generate an aura of unapproachabil-ity. Even at office hours, students are often surprised upon arrival by questions such as, "What are you doing here?" and "Can you come next week? I'm really busy now trying to meet a deadline for my grant." It is no wonder that in a large classroom setting, students are reluctant to respond even to the simplest question. In an effort to put at least a small dent in this barrier, I attempt to get things rolling on the first day of class by telling my audience that I am available and open to invitations for coffee, lunch, a game of tennis, and almost anything else they might suggest. Moreover, such invitations will gain them an "A for the day," which amounts to a few undefined number of points. Generally about 15 of 300 students take me up on this opportunity at some point during the course. I have no idea what I would do if all 300 ever responded.

Sarah approached me immediately after the first class and asked if I was serious about my invitation to play music. I had mentioned that I played the violin and she wondered whether I would like to play the Bach Double Violin Concerto with her. As with many science majors, Sarah was also an avid musician. I gladly accepted her invitation and we practiced together throughout the entire ten week quarter. By that time, it was starting to sound pretty good, at least to our ears. Then Sarah shocked me with her request to perform the piece for the entire class on the last day. This Biology course was held in a large auditorium with a stage, and there were over 400 biology majors in it, mostly serious pre-meds. Without giving it any thought, I agreed to the performance.

I have never been so scared in a classroom setting as in the moments shortly before we played the first note. It suddenly occurred to me that this was me on stage with a violin in my hand, not with the usual microphone and visual aids for my lecture. Why was I doing this? What would the students think? At 7:55 a.m., Sarah and I began our duet as the 400 silently drifted in and took their seats. I was too dazed to notice them, but soon the glorious sounds of Bach took complete control of my senses and nothing else mattered.

When we finished, the ovation was deafening. I was amazed at the response. We bowed, Sarah took a seat, and the lecture began, but this time it felt very different.

I wondered why my students enjoyed this performance so much. Our artistry was certainly not the reason. What I learned from discussions with several of the students was that they appreciated seeing me in a different light from that of the usual Biology teacher. I had opened myself up to them, exposing my human side and my vulnerability, and I had joined this venture as an equal together with one of their fellow students. Without planning it, I had attained my long sought after goal of breaking down the barriers between student and professor. I think Carl Rogers would have been pleased.

Matt is a good example of how my invitations for extra-curricular activities led to a mentor/mentee relationship and even to a change in careers. Answering my call in class for the need for a tennis doubles partner, this thin, somewhat frail looking young Russian immigrant joined me and two of my teaching assistants (TAs) on the court during the first week of my non-majors course. Along with the considerable chutzpah needed for playing tennis with his teachers, Matt also displayed surprising skill. Due to his lack of tennis etiquette, however, he did not exactly endear himself to me or my TAs, and we did not invite him to join us again. We lost touch until the following year when Matt appeared in my course for Biology majors. Once again he turned up on the tennis court, this time with considerably better manners. As a result of his interest in my course for non-majors taken during his freshman year, Matt had decided to change majors from Economics to Molecular Biology.

During his remaining years at UCSD, we often played tennis together, and this led to a mutually enjoyable relationship. I hired Matt as a TA for two of my courses, and he was a big help to me and also was greatly appreciated by the students. Matt was an unusually good listener, and he loved to hear stories about my life as well as my research, often amazing me with his uncanny recollection of small details even years later. As the years and tennis games went by, Matt gradually grew sufficiently close and confident to confide in me about his personal life as well as his academic experiences. With tennis serving as a starting point, I played a significant role in helping Matt define his career. I am sure this scholarly young man will eventually become an outstanding scientist and devoted teacher.

Stefan was another non-major who accepted my offer to meet on the tennis court. An Economics major and not a pre-med, it seemed that he was not doing this for the sake of a letter of recommendation, but rather simply to improve his game and get to know me. Each time we played, I won easily, but notwithstanding his deficiencies on the court, Stefan promised to beat me the next time. We always had an enjoyable conversation after the game, sharing ideas from books we had read among many other topics. He was widely read, with an excellent memory and obviously very intelligent.

Several years after Stefan graduated and left UCSD, he finally requested a letter from me in connection with his application to graduate school. Knowing him so well, I was able to write a glowing recommendation, but added one criticism. I said that "Stefan was not always honest. He often promised to beat me in tennis, but never did." The reviewers must have gotten a chuckle out of that "criticism." I would like to think that it helped his application stand out among the hundreds of others they reviewed. Not only was Stefan accepted to this highly prestigious graduate program, he was also awarded a scholarship.

Even when students do meet with me one on one, although I try my best, it is nevertheless impossible to establish a true equality. In point of fact, we are not equal. My age, experience, and title cause almost every student to treat me respectfully, referring to me as Professor or Dr. Green no matter how often I ask them to call me by my first name, which is how I address them. But certain activities, such as playing tennis and music, are great equalizers, especially at my amateurish level. Students whom I have engaged in such extra-curricular activities have generally maintained contact with me for many years after completion of the course. It is especially these students who have brought about my greatest sense of joy in teaching.

I don't consider the relationships that develop with my students as true friendships, but they do lead often to my serving as their mentor and/or role model. A true friendship demands a mutual feeling of equality, and as I already explained, this cannot exist with my students. I would never call on a student in time of need or distress, for example. However, I always treat them with respect, and that creates a feeling of trust and openness. As a mentor, I try to spend much more time listening than talking, which is not easy for a professor. There is a great tendency when being with a student to go on and on telling stories about our lives and our research. But a good mentor has to be willing to listen to their mentees' concerns about all sorts of things, from academic to social life. Providing a good ear and a suggestion every once in a while is the essence of serving the mentee well.

I have been told by a few people that my invitations to meet with students for activities outside of my office are highly unprofessional. One reason for this is that it could lead to my playing favorites when it comes to grades. I am positive that this is not the case because my TAs grade all of the exams, and final grades are based entirely on those points. My **feeling** is that the interactions I had with students because of these invitations resulted in the most significant teaching and mentoring experiences of my entire career. Furthermore, UCSD is very supportive of professors making an effort to interact in every possible way with their students. The "Dine with a Prof" program goes as far as paying for lunches anywhere on campus, including the exclusive Faculty Club. Unfortunately, student-professor interactions still happen all too rarely, even with a free lunch.

Near the end of each course, the students are asked to complete a professor evaluation survey. Among the favorites I have received is the following, complete with grammatical errors. I was 70 years of age at the time it was written.

"Theres no way Dr. Green is 87 years old thats bs. He's probably 60 years old, and he plays tennis like if he's 30. He's just a hustler making us think he's so old so we can challenge him in tennis then get embarrassed."

2.

CREATIVITY AND COURAGE

Although research scientists are generally very hard-working, highly intelligent people, not all that many make the major discoveries that can be considered truly ground-breaking. Most keep busy within their field of specialization throughout their entire careers, adding small bits of information to an ever-enlarging monumental question using the same techniques they mastered early in their careers. There are not many Einsteins out there. But does one have to be an Einstein to be creative? What is really meant by the term "creativity?"

In his inspiring work, "The Courage to Create," Rollo May partially defines creativity as "the encounter of the intensively conscious human being with his or her world." I say "partially" because earlier Dr. May refers to Webster's definition of creativity as "basically the process of making, of bringing into being." Merging these two definitions, we see that creativity is the process of bringing something into being by the intensively conscious human being's encounter with his or her world. The intense person's encounter with the world in itself creates nothing.

According to Dr. May, creativity cannot exist without some form of courage. Whereas I do not believe that creativity **always** demands some form of courage, the following stories illustrate the creativity and courage of two of my former graduate students, Bill Hayward and Susumu Tonegawa, as well as my own. In 1964 Bill and Susumu were the first two pre-doctoral candidates to join my laboratory for thesis research. Their intense encounters with very difficult research questions can be thought of as a type of courage because both could have chosen a far less tortuous path to a successful career. Without such courage, however, not nearly as creative a product would have resulted from their work.

Unlike the stereotypical Southern California surfer dude, there was nothing in Bill's appearance that would cause one to think of him as anything but a nerdy scholar. A graduate of UC Riverside, Bill had never strayed far from home, nor had he any desire to do so. The new UC campus in San Diego, with its ideal climate, suited him perfectly. Shortly after starting his graduate work, only 23 years of age, Bill married his childhood sweetheart and settled in a small home in La Jolla near the ocean. Unlike many of our students, Bill cared little for the ocean. His activities were confined to working night and day in the lab, at least 70 hours per week, with an occasional evening left free for playing poker with his friends. The long hours in the lab were typical for graduate students in the '60's, at least for those in the natural sciences.

Well into his fifth year, Bill had solved several problems and had published a few papers. He had come close to answering a very esoteric question, but there was no known way at the time to solve this problem. The question concerned the mechanism whereby the lambda virus repressor acted to block lambda virus RNA synthesis, i.e., transcription. There were two possibilities: the repressor either prevented the enzyme, RNA polymerase, from binding to the viral DNA, or it allowed the enzyme to bind, but not copy the DNA. This was the typical kind of question that Molecular Biologists were working on at that time. Having no idea how to answer this question, and given the fact that Bill had already devoted so much time to his thesis, I advised him to stop work in the lab and write his thesis. To my surprise, Bill refused my offer. He said he wouldn't leave until he had solved this problem.

It occurred to me that perhaps Bill was having too good a time living in La Jolla, even on his meager graduate student stipend. Why else would he want to continue working on an insoluble problem? I got him to send off an application for a post-doctoral position at the Rockefeller Institute (now University) in New York city, and he was quickly accepted. Nevertheless, this idealistic young man was determined to stay on with me until he had answered the question completely.

Worried that Bill might spend years getting nowhere, I began thinking about his research problem very intensively. Surely there must be some way to answer it, but nothing came to mind for several weeks. Then the strangest experience of my entire career occurred. I dreamed of three consecutive experiments that would answer the question definitively. I jumped out of bed in the pitch darkness and raced to the dresser where I kept a pen and pad of paper. Without turning on a light or putting on my glasses, seeing nothing that is, I scribbled a brief note for each of the experiments, then went back to sleep. Because I kept the lights off, it seemed like I had never awakened.

Upon awaking in the morning, I laughed at what I imagined to be my nonsensical dream. I couldn't wait to see what I had written in the dark, thinking that I probably wouldn't even be able to decipher it. But surprisingly, it was legible to me at least, and more than that, it was logical and might actually work. I realize that the following description of my dream is far too much scientific detail for non-biologists to comprehend, but I present it to emphasize the complexity of my dream.

First, add Rifamycin to the lambda virus infected E. coli lambda lysogenic cells and wait until transcription stops. Rifamycin was known to block RNA synthesis, but permit RNA polymerase to bind to the start sites on DNA. Then heat inactivate the lambda virus repressor. Second, isolate the lambda DNA-RNA polymerase complex, as we had done previously, and dialyze away the Rifamycin. The dialysis step had never been done before, but it was needed in order to remove the Rifamycin from the enzyme. Third, assay lambda virus transcription by the complex. If the repressor blocks attachment of the enzyme to lambda DNA, there would be no RNA synthesis. In contrast, if the repressor permitted the enzyme to bind but not transcribe the DNA, lambda RNA would be synthesized. The solution was just that simple, at least after the dream.

Unlike Archimedes, I dressed before racing off to the lab to tell Bill my incredible dream. If the dialysis step would work, these three dreamed up experiments would answer the question and Bill could finish his thesis. Calm and efficient as always, he proceeded at once with the work and in only a week proved definitively that the lambda repressor blocked RNA polymerase from binding to the viral DNA. Bill never told me whether he believed me about this being a dream, but he was certainly happy to finish his thesis research so quickly. He soon left for New York, enjoyed a very successful career there, and never returned to sunny California.

I consider this the most creative research of my career, and feel that the intensity of my encounter with the question led to the answer occurring to me in a dream. Bill provided the courage with his decision to carry on with the project until it was finished. It could have taken years, and there were no guarantees that it would ever be completed. So much for text book definitions of the so-called "scientific method." I prefer dreams.

There is no doubt that the founding chairman of the Biology Department at UCSD, Dr. David Bonner, had considerable courage and creativity. He wanted his department to focus exclusively on molecular approaches to all fields in the biological sciences. This included Genetics, Botany, Developmental Biology, and even Ecology. With considerable opposition from senior biologists already present at the Scripps Institute of Oceanography, Bonner recruited faculty and graduate students who fit into his plans. David correctly realized, unlike some of his opponents from the SIO faculty, that Molecular Biology was not just a "passing fad that would soon disappear."

One of Dr. Bonner's first recruited graduate students was Susumu Tonegawa. A graduate of Nagoya University in 1963, he was considered the best student in his class. As I was the only Molecular Biologist in the department at the time, it was my good fortune that Susumu decided to do his thesis research with me. I say good fortune mainly because I so much enjoyed getting to know him. He taught me some things about Japanese culture, and he became more like a friend than one of my students. However, neither as a student in my Virology course nor as a researcher did Susumu seem any better than most of the other graduate students at UCSD. He was certainly very hard working and bright, but so were the others. After a little more than a year in my lab, I said to him, "So far you've only done the experiments I have suggested. When are you going to think of some experiments yourself?" I expected my students to show some creativity, not simply act as technicians.

Not long after that, Susumu left my lab and continued his thesis work with Prof. Masaki Hayashi, a friend from my graduate school whom I had helped recruit. I was somewhat hurt by this, but not angry because I assumed that Susumu felt more comfortable working under the guidance of a Japanese professor. In due time, he completed his doctoral thesis, then went on to do post-doctoral research at the nearby Salk Institute under the supervision of Dr. Renato Dulbecco, the same virologist I had done my post-doctoral work with while he was at Cal Tech. Up until this point, Susumu displayed no signs of conducting any research out of the ordinary.

When it came time to strike out on his own, Dr. Tonegawa heeded Dulbecco's advice to take a position at the Immunology Institute in Basel, Switzerland. Although he knew virtually nothing about the field of Immunology, Susumu had the courage not only to go alone to a country that was not exactly welcoming to foreigners, but also to take on a very hot project that many Immunologists all over the world were attempting to solve. In essence, the question was, "How do we humans have a sufficient number of genes to code for all the antibodies we need for recognizing nearly every foreign substance that can enter our blood?" This "antibody diversity" question was of obvious importance to every biologist, but the means to answer it was far from clear.

Susumu worked on this difficult question alone for two years, racing many other labs that had more than twenty researchers in them. Using the DNA-RNA hybridization techniques that he had learned in my laboratory while a graduate student, as well as some procedures that he conceived of, Susumu was the first to answer this question. During this time of intensive research he published nothing, and as a result, he received a notice terminating his employment in Basel. Fortunately, he either ignored the notice or didn't notice it until after completing his work. Susumu Tonegawa received a well-deserved Nobel Prize for this creative research in 1987.

The question in my mind is, When did Tonegawa become creative? I saw no sign of his creativity before he left for Switzerland, although perhaps others did. It seems clear that his courage to attack a very important, difficult project with a great deal of intensity was in large part the basis for his creative work that led to the Nobel Prize. But what if, even with all his courage and intensity, he had not been the first to answer the question? Had he never published his findings because of not being first, would he now be considered a creative scientist? Creativity is clearly not easy to define or determine. Whether or not it depends on courage, sometimes it may also require some luck, or perhaps even a dream.

3.

SHAKEN DREAMS

It was Spring, 1965, and I was still a very unattached young man. In fact, I can't recall having gone out on one date since the previous summer. My research was keeping me very busy, as usual, and now I was scheduled to teach Virology for the first time to undergraduates. Preparation for this course had taken an inordinate amount of time and effort, what with having to read all the journal articles from the past several years and then deciding which ones to include. Only twenty students signed up for this elective, and I planned to have a discussion based format rather than formal lectures. The small room in Bonner Hall that was assigned for this course was ideal for this style of teaching.

After a few weeks, I couldn't help but notice one young lady in the class for several reasons. First, members of this "species," i.e., females, were still quite rare on the campus, regardless of appearance. Second, this member was gorgeous…an Audrey Hepburn look-alike. Third, and most significant, Myra actually seemed to show some interest not only in Virology, but in me as well. Naturally I found this hard to fathom for several reasons. First, I was an "old man" of 28, and she couldn't have been more than 22. Second, I was her teacher after all, and girls didn't fall for their teachers, did they? Third … well their must be many other reasons why this just couldn't happen … not to me anyway.

The basis for my admittedly hopeful fantasy lay in the observation that after class, Myra would stay behind to ask me some questions about viruses. Of course she may actually have been excited about the subject, or perhaps she needed more explanation about the complex experiments that had been discussed. Her questions were always intelligent, and her interest appeared genuine. Nevertheless, there was something about her way of looking at me, perhaps her stance being so near, and those beautiful dark brown eyes peering into my heart. But then, satisfied by my explanations, she would depart all too abruptly and I would chalk it up to wishful thinking on my part.

By week eight, I was convinced that this was nothing but the total foolishness of a desperately lonely professor. Even though her questions had persisted every day after class, nothing more had transpired. What did I think was going to happen? How could I have such foolish thoughts? Once again all the other students had left the classroom and Myra was asking her questions when, all of a sudden she reached out and took hold of my hand. She came closer than ever and, looking deeply into my eyes, asked her first question unrelated to Virology. "Do you feel something?" My heart skipped a few beats, started pounding rapidly, then stopped. "Yes, I certainly do," I eagerly replied. We stood there holding hands tightly, not saying another word as Bonner Hall began to sway back and forth.

When the earthquake finally came to a halt after what seemed an eternity, Myra quickly took her leave without any further questions. I had never felt so shaken. For all intents and purposes, my course, like the quake, had run its course.

MATCHMAKING

There were many times when I would get to know a student on a more personal level and discover that he or she was feeling rather lonely. You might wonder how anyone can feel lonely in a university setting, but it is not uncommon for someone to feel much lonelier in a crowd than when alone. I have often noticed this when dining in a student cafeteria, where I seem to be the only one sitting alone in this thriving throng of commotion. It is well documented that students' grades often suffer when they are having social problems, and loneliness is among the most usually cited.

The lecture hall was jammed to capacity with 350 eager students, mostly eager to get this class finished. It was the first week after the long summer vacation and everyone had better things to do than listen to a Biology lecture. In a large classroom setting like this, many students never meet a single person during the entire 10 week quarter. I decided to begin the class with an exercise I had learned in an encounter group. I told the students that, at the count of three, everyone should turn around and shake hands with the student directly behind him or her. Without hesitation I counted to three and said "Turn around." They did as they were instructed by their well-meaning instructor, only to confront the back of the person in the row behind. After the laughter died down, I pretended that I knew this was going to happen, and told them that this was an example of the difficulty in getting to know one another in such a large class.

For years I assumed this effort at breaking down barriers in a large classroom had been a total failure. Then one day while visiting a local biotech company, a young man approached with a big smile. "Hi Professor Green. You don't remember me, but I had your course about ten years ago, and I'll never forget that day when you told us to turn around and shake hands with the person behind you. I was very shy, but with reluctance I did it and met the girl seated behind me. We're married now and have two kids. I owe it all to you."

Of course it doesn't always go this well. Barry was one of my most popular TAs. Tall and very good looking, his discussion section was over-subscribed, and many more students were still trying to get into it even several weeks after the course began…mostly girls for some obvious reason. I knew one such aspirant because she worked at the Grove coffee shop, which was my favorite at the time. Allie confided to me that she was "dying to meet Barry, but simply didn't have the nerve." I was certain that Allie, tall, dark, beautiful, and very intellectual, was the perfect match for Barry. While waiting with Barry for our coffees to be prepared, I concocted a scheme for their meeting. Instead of having us come to the counter for our coffees, which was the usual procedure, Allie should bring the drinks to our table where I would casually introduce her to Barry. Very reluctantly, she agreed to do this, but she was obviously extremely nervous. After an unusually long wait, Allie finally appeared. She set my espresso on our table, then tripped over the leg of the table, spilling Barry's hot coffee all over his pants. The scene was like a typical Hollywood movie, hilarious and sad at the same time. Muttering profound apologies, Allie raced off to the back of the shop where she remained out of sight for the duration of our stay, and probably much longer. To my dismay, this unfortunate event was their only meeting, and Allie laid all the blame on me.

Another subtle effort at match making occurred while eating lunch with Don in a student cafeteria. Don was a very outgoing, somewhat brash young man who seemed to enjoy my company for some reason. While telling him one of my million stories, I noticed that he was looking over my shoulder and no longer listening to me. Casually I turned around and discovered the reason for this rude behavior. Two attractive girls were at a table behind me, both smoking while eating lunch. I interrupted my story at once, realizing that Don hadn't heard a word of it anyway, and grabbed his attention by saying, "How would you like to meet those girls? Why don't you just go up to them and ask what it would take to get them to stop smoking? Tell them that you and Professor Green are conducting a campus survey about how to stop smoking." He loved the idea and scooted over to them before I could even blink.

When Don returned, he had a big grin all over his face, two phone numbers and a weekend lined up. And I had the idea for starting a student organization. It would be named Club BioMed, a variation of Club Med in name only, and it would focus on teaching college and high school students about cancer. Of course, the harmful effects of smoking would be a major component in the lecture. Don was very helpful in getting the club started, and he became its first president. In addition to teaching young people about cancer and the harmful effects of smoking, the club had many other advantages, including social. I think starting Club BioMed was my main contribution to students along social lines, although many more direct approaches were attempted over the years. My efforts were rewarded with a title : the "match-making professor."

5.

CLASSROOM COMMUNICATION

From the time I began teaching large introductory biology classes in 1972, communicating with undergraduates in the lecture hall became increasingly difficult. Even in small classes with less than 50 students, my courses were rated as good, but not outstanding. I assumed this was due to the need to improve my lectures, so I contacted a teaching specialist, Dr. John Andrews. After many discussions and videotapes of my lectures, there was still no discernible improvement in ratings. Finally, like any respectable scientist, I devised an experiment. I prepared a lecture as best I could on a topic I loved and knew thoroughly, then presented it to a small class of 30 students. After the lecture, I handed out a questionnaire that asked things such as: "Was the lecture clear? Was the instructor well prepared? Did the instructor understand the topic? Was the lecture well organized?

To my amazement, a subset of the students rated me very poorly on all of these questions, whereas most rated me very highly. Overall, my rating for this one lecture was good, but not outstanding. From this experiment, I surmised there was nothing more to be done about my lectures. Improved ratings would depend on some factor in my teaching other than the lecture.

Years later, I learned what this was. Convincing the students that I cared about them was the most critical factor, not how well I lectured. Meanwhile, before arriving at this now obvious conclusion, I tried a variety of methods to go beyond the formal lecture in an effort to stimulate student minds in a large classroom setting. I always felt that there was far more to teaching than merely presenting the facts in a lecture. The following are a few examples of such efforts, as well as some misunderstandings that resulted from my good intentions.

Language is rapidly evolving, and young people are most responsible for this. They are first to utilize advances in technology, wherein lies a whole new vocabulary. When I saw the movie, "Clueless," I realized that all too often I had no clue what these Valley girls were talking about. How could I communicate with my class if I didn't speak their language? So I asked one of my TAs to view this movie and explain to me the new language. When I flashed the "Whatever" sign in response to a comment made by a student in class, my efforts were rewarded with an ovation. I was one of them instantly, not some geek behind a podium. After class, Naren, one of my TAs, smiled at me and said, "Wassup Professor."

My favorite question, which I asked on the first day of just about every Introductory Biology course, was "What is living?" Note that I said "living," not "life." I knew this question was somewhat ambiguous, but that was intentional. I wanted the students to do some thinking. My all time favorite answer was, "I just came back from a great skiing trip, and that's what I call living." Most often, to my amazed disappointment, students would reply with one word answers such as, "Breathing," and "Reproducing," and other properties of living things. I would then try to restrain myself from insulting the respondent by giving examples of how their answer was incomplete at best. "Plants are living, but they don't breathe. The mule is incapable of reproducing. Hold your breath for a few seconds. You're still alive, right?" They would soon try using a few more words in their answers, eventually listing the properties of all living things. I would then get them to realize that there were exceptions to all of these properties of living things. For example, most living cells are able to divide, but not neurons, red blood cells, and other terminally differentiated cells. When they finally arrived at the cell as the basic building block of all living things, I asked them about viruses, which are not cells and can only reproduce when inside a living cell. I always loved it when they said viruses were not living because they could not reproduce by themselves. "Can you?" I asked.

The second lecture was about the molecules present in all cells. I would start by asking students to name a protein found in human cells. To my great surprise, very few students would even venture a guess. They would just sit there, waiting for me to answer my own question. But to their surprise, I just stood there not saying a word. The silence seemed awkward, but I would not give in to their lazy minds. Once when the silence became unbearable, a student finally raised her hand. Relieved, I called on her and she responded with the word "Chicken?" My mouth must have opened very wide, but I did my best not to insult her. I presumed she thought chicken proteins became human after we eat them, so I replied, "Chicken is not only protein, you know. The skin is mostly fat." The boy next to her immediately shouted out, "How about tuna fish? No fat there." The final shock to my system came when another student asked whether these classroom discussions would be included on the exams. Teachers can learn a lot from using the Socratic approach. I learned some new "human" proteins.

There were a few other times when my responses to student comments did not show kindness or understanding, even when well intentioned. In fact, in my early days of teaching, my reputation for caustic replies was all too well known. Once when I was lecturing on the structure of the biological membrane, the so-called fluid mosaic membrane discovered by my colleague, Jon Singer, and his pre-doctoral student, Garth Nicolson, I went to great lengths to explain that the membrane surrounding the cell is a bilayer comprised of two layers of phospholipid molecules. In contrast, some organelles, such as the nucleus and mitochondria, are actually surrounded by two separate membranes, and thus have four layers of phospholipid molecules around them. A hand quickly shot up, so I stopped my lecture and called on the young lady to whom it belonged. "I don't understand how you got four layers of molecules around the mitochondria," she asked. Without hesitating to think for a moment, I answered, "I just spent a long time going into this. If you don't understand why 2 plus 2 equals 4, please stop by my office and I'll explain it to you in more detail." The class roared with laughter, the girl turned bright red, and I immediately realized that I had said the wrong thing. Fortunately, I never heard from that student again or I might still be in court.

I like starting off my lectures with something totally off the wall just to get the students to relax and pay attention. Often I would use a line from one of the Monty Python movies. Two of my favorites were "Run away" and "Not dead yet." The latter was generally used to poke fun at myself whenever an opportunity arose. This is undoubtedly the safest form of humor. In my lecture on aging, the students always laughed when I used the skin on the back of my own hand to show the lack of elasticity that occurs with increasing age due to collagen cross-linking. I had to slap my hand to get the skin to settle back down. Humor, when used appropriately, really spices up a lecture. One of my favorite student evaluations said, "Dr. Green is the only professor who can show the relationship between Biology and Monty Python."

Once I tried to teach my class how important it was to gain their attention right at the start of lecture. If this didn't happen, it was likely that they could be lost in space for the entire class period. To illustrate my point, I began the lecture with this sentence: "A good speaker must start off each lecture with a hooker." As the class roared with laughter, I realized that I had meant to say "with a hook." I couldn't have possibly come up with a better one, so I dropped the subject immediately and proceeded with the lecture. I really had their attention.

However, there were times when my humor was not appropriate. Generally, this occurred when I said or did something wrong without trying to be funny. Once I came to class with a Beavis and Butthead clicker in my pocket, right next to the microphone. Given to me by one of my teaching assistants, it produced the voices of these TV cartoon characters uttering their commonly heard sayings. So when a student asked me a question, it came as a great shock to hear Beavis respond, loud and clear, "Shut up dumb ass." I had accidentally pushed a button that produced that response. Everyone looked around the room attempting to determine where the voice had come from, while I acted as innocent as possible, trying my best to keep from cracking up.

Another time I started off the class by doing tricks with a yo-yo. I had been pretty good as a kid, winning many yo-yos in contests before the 7th grade. My students were enjoying seeing me "walk the dog" and "rock the baby in the cradle," but then in total innocence I said, "I'll bet you never saw a professor play with his yo-yo in class before." They were all in hysterics while I pretended not to notice that I had said anything out of the ordinary.

6.

ACADEMIC HONESTY

Most universities operate under a code of ethics referred to as the "honor system." As every student knows, this is where the university has no system and the students have no honor. There is no question that cheating in school is a serious and common problem. It is also impressive how much ingenuity and creative energy goes into this activity. If even a small fraction of such energy were used in studying, far less cheating would occur. Some of the more creative methods I have encountered include:

1. changing the answers and submitting the exam for a regrade;

2. going to the restroom during the exam and having a cheat sheet taped inside one of the stalls;

3. never turning in the exam and claiming the TAs lost it while grading, thus deserving a makeup exam.

Only once in all my years of teaching did a student request that his score be lowered due to an error in grading. I was astounded by such honesty, and after getting up off the floor, I told him to be sure to see me whenever he needed a letter of recommendation. Not surprisingly, he also got an A in my course.

Shortly after returning from my fabulous sabbatical year in London in 1971, I was informed by the Chairman of Biology, Herbert Stern, that I would have to teach an introductory level course in the spring. Called Natural Science 2E, this course was the fifth in a sequence preceded by courses in Chemistry and Physics. It was designed for the Revelle College students, all supposedly brilliant. It would be the first time I taught a class with more than 25 students, this one with a projected enrollment of 350, and the first time I taught a general biology course. The course was expected to include lectures in the areas of Biochemistry, Cell Biology, Molecular Biology, Classical Mendelian Genetics, and Modern Genetics. Having majored in Chemistry and

Biochemistry for all my degrees, I knew very little about cell biology and almost nothing about Mendelian and modern genetics. The idea of lecturing to a very large audience, especially about subjects I knew little about, was terrifying.

Fortunately I had two quarters in which to prepare lectures, and I also managed to recruit a few guest lecturers for the Genetics sections. With such a large class size, I was permitted to have 25 upper division TAs assigned. I actually knew very few of them, so I had to base my selections on their written applications. The main criteria were their grade point average and prior course work. There was no time for interviews, but even if there had been, I doubt whether that would have prevented the horrendous mess that occurred.

After a shaky start to my lectures, even without any earthquakes, the course started to run fairly smoothly. After only four weeks, it was nearly time for the midterm exam. I devoted a tremendous amount of time and effort preparing it, trying to include every major topic covered in the lectures. When it was completed, I decided to show it to all of the TAs for their input. It seemed to me that this would be a good learning experience for them, as well as providing me with their feedback. I assumed my TAs had a better sense than I of what was too hard or easy for students at that level. After receiving their comments at a meeting, I had my secretary type up the final version of the exam and run off 400 copies. It was now Thursday afternoon, and the exam was scheduled for early the next morning. What a relief it was to have completed this task on time.

What followed was one of the most difficult situations I ever faced during my 46 years at UCSD. At 5:00 pm, three of my TAs came to my office with the awful news that one of the TAs had shown the entire exam to his section. Now that 20 of the students had seen it, and perhaps many more had been told about it, what could be done to make this a fair exam? Even delaying the exam and creating a new one would not be fair because I had included just about every topic on this one, and seeing the questions in advance would definitely provide an advantage. After a lengthy discussion, we arrived at the decision to make it a take-home exam over the weekend. Students could use their books, but at least they would learn what I felt was important by completing this test. I could think of no fair alternative. Totally upset by this unfortunate turn of events, I looked forward to confronting Thomas, the TA who was responsible for my agony.

The students were of course shocked to hear what had happened, but were not at all disappointed when told that they could complete the exam at home over the weekend. The next day, Saturday, I flew to New York for a one week conference at Cold Spring Harbor, where I was presenting a paper on my research. The TAs had the responsibility of grading the exams during that week. On Tuesday I received a phone call from my secretary informing me of the "crisis." Approximately 20 students had gone to the Revelle College Provost's office demanding that the exam be discarded because some students had cheated by collaborating. Without consulting me, the Provost had told these students that he would insist that I discard the exam. Furthermore, he wanted me to return to La Jolla immediately and deal with this situation. I calmly replied that I would return when the meeting ended, and that the Provost had no right telling the students what I would do. As a tenured professor, I felt very confident that I had done the right thing, and that no one was going to tell me how to run my course.

I stayed at the meeting the entire week, growing more and more concerned about the revolution taking place back home. Upon my return, I learned from my TAs that nearly 75% of the students had received A's on the exam, most of the rest got B's, and there were a small number of lower grades. Armed with this information, I went to the Provost's office and listened impatiently to his story about the student invasion of his office. I then presented him with a very logical argument. "How many students do you think would march on your office if I threw out the exam, given that 75% of the 350 students had worked hard enough over the weekend to receive an A?" It only required some simple arithmetic to estimate the number at 200. Being a chemist, he quickly got my point and backed down from his demand. An apology was too much to expect, but at least I felt relieved. I had feared far worse consequences.

I next confronted Thomas, the TA who had given out the exam to his section. He had already been reprimanded by the Dean of Students, his cheating had been entered into his academic record, and he was prohibited from ever serving as a TA again. When I asked him why he had shown the exam to his section, he provided a very simple and logical explanation:

"I thought this was the best way possible to prepare my students for your exam." This simpleton simply wanted to be my best TA by helping all his students get an A. Even though his cheating had nearly ruined my course, I could not scream at him as I had expected to do, or even offer an argument. For once, I was speechless. This well meaning young man, an undergraduate himself, was "just trying to help my students."

Although so many of the students received an A on the exam, not everyone was happy about it, however. A few students actually complained that I had "ruined their weekend." Getting an A didn't seem to make that much of a difference to them. My wife's brother, Jerry, was one of the angry students in this class. Coming from Ecuador, he was a Freshman with a major in Economics, taking Biology only because it was a Revelle College requirement. Jerry had been one of the few students who had not realized he could use the text book on that infamous exam, so he didn't get an A on it or for the course. In fact, mine was one of only two courses in which Jerry got less than an A during his entire undergraduate years at UCSD.

Seven years later, after I entered into a serious relationship with Lynn, she phoned Jerry in Chicago to determine whether he knew me, and if so, what he thought of me. Still disgruntled about my course after all those years, he told Lynn, "Our relationship can only improve." But like a good scientist, Lynn trusted her own observations more than her brother's, and we got married within the year. My relationship with Jerry has definitely improved.

7.

Responsibility

I was doing an experiment in my friend Milton Saier's lab when a former student appeared. Maryam was an extremely attractive Persian girl, bordering on knock 'em dead gorgeous. In no time, several of Saier's students gathered around us, not to learn about my experiment. She came to find out whether she could serve as a TA for my next course, which was coming up in a few weeks. In my usual kidding around manner, but feeling somewhat disturbed from my work, I replied that she would first have to answer a few questions. "Tell me the name of one molecule that is inside the nucleus of a cell." Maryam looked at me with wide eyes, but didn't say a word. I quickly simplified the question to, "Forget about the nucleus. Just tell me the name of any molecule inside of a cell." This time her mouth dropped open, her eyes grew even wider, and still she said nothing. "What's the matter?" I asked. "To tell the truth," she murmured, "I didn't know molecules could fit inside a cell."

I should have said goodbye to her right then and there, but I guess I was too shocked to know what to say or do. This was the simplest question in the world, and Maryam had received an A in my course last quarter. I had just been joking around by asking her that question, but her response was so ridiculous that I didn't believe my ears. More importantly, I didn't trust my own judgment, so I told her to fill out the application for becoming a TA.

One of Dr. Saier's undergraduate researchers, Bart, had been listening in on this spur of the moment oral exam. When I told him how shocked I was by Maryam's answers, he rushed to her defense. "You were really hard on her putting her on the spot like that. She probably just got very nervous." I assumed Bart was struck dumb by Maryam's good looks, but because she got an A in my course, I went against my instinct and accepted her as a TA.

Within a few weeks after the start of my course, I began receiving emails from students saying that Maryam either couldn't answer, or refused to answer, their questions. Later I heard that she was not even showing up for some of her discussion sections. This was intolerable, so I set up a meeting with her in my office.

In response to why she had not attended some of her sections, Maryam simply replied, "I know some other TAs who also don't show up for them. Why are you picking only on me?" Trying my best to remain rational, I told her what to me at least was obvious. She had a responsibility as a TA to attend her sections. This was a paid position...a job, and what other TAs did should have been of no concern to her. She must learn to take responsibility for her own actions and stop trying to place the blame on others.

Her response to my logic was only a flood of tears followed by more nonsense about the other TAs. By now I realized what a mistake I had made by hiring her as a TA. I should have trusted my first impression that resulted from the "oral exam" in the lab. I can only imagine how Maryam managed to get an A in my course, and I pray that this pre-medical student never became a doctor. I can hear her saying, "Why didn't the other doctor stop the bleeding?"

8.

GRADES

One of the most difficult aspects of being a teacher is the necessity of assigning grades. Along with this tedious chore comes the preparation of new exams each term, followed closely by the boring task of grading them. Despite the strong urging of the Biology Department for a Gaussian curved distribution of grades, centering on C, I stuck to my preferred method throughout my entire 46 years of teaching at UCSD.

The curve system of grading is completely opposite to my philosophy in that it presupposes a certain fraction of students must fail the course and an equal number must receive an A. My system can be described as an "adjusted sliding scale." The top score, or the average of the top few scores in a very large class, is set equal to 100%, and at least 85% of that is an A grade. From 72% to 84% is a B, 55% to 71% a C, 40% to 54% a D, and lower than 40% is an F. By this method, theoretically at least, everyone in the class can receive an A. This made students very happy, at least before they took the first exam. It added to their incentive to do well, and it reduced their feeling the need to compete. Of course, there were always those few pre-meds who felt a great need to compete, wanting to be the only one in the class to receive an A+.

In this regard, the most memorable example was Stan. I was having coffee one afternoon at the Grove with a few of my students when I heard a voice from off in the distance: "Hey Dr. Green! Did you say we could get an A in your course if we beat you in tennis?" "Come closer so I can see who you are," I replied. As he approached, I realized it was Stan, the number one player on the UCSD tennis team. I had seen him play for the team, and realized I would certainly prove no competition for him. He must have realized this, too. I was sure that's why he changed my class comment offering an A for the day to an A for the course. It also occurred to me that he made the comment from where I would not recognize him. An A for the day amounted merely to a few points, serving the purpose of breaking the barrier between professor and student.

I agreed to play doubles with Stan, but not singles. We each got a member of the team for our partners and had a close, enjoyable game. My greatest pleasure came when I aced Stan on my very first serve and saw his jaw drop open in speechless amazement. I was also pleased that Stan didn't ask me for any points in the course when his team won the match. But he annoyed me once again soon after the final exam. Stan was playing on a court two removed from mine when he shouted to me, "Your final was too easy!" I discussed this with him a few months later when he came for a letter of recommendation for medical school. He was actually upset that so many students received an A in my class. In all my years of teaching, Stan was the only student who ever lodged that complaint. Needless to say, I wasn't too high in my praise for this super-competitive guy.

No matter where the lines are drawn for each letter grade, in a class of 300 students there will always be quite a few border-line cases. At my discretion, I assigned plus and minus grades for those, depending on some well defined variables that enabled me to justify my decisions when and if necessary. I realize that grades play an important role in the lives of many students, especially the pre-meds. However, it was extremely difficult to deal with the complaining and begging that took place year after year. I'm very sorry if this appears sexist on my part, but I can honestly say that it was almost exclusively girls who arrived in my office after receiving their final grades. The boys argued for points on the exams, but not usually for their final grade, perhaps because they were already too busy getting drunk.

The usual plea made by the girls went something like, "I studied so hard for this course and only got a B. Isn't there something extra I can do to get a few more points that I need for an A?" I would respond with my usual "What do you have in mind?" Although this made it seem like I was being open to the possibility, I was actually looking forward to hearing some creative answers. When the student would offer to do some extra credit work, either oral or written, I explained that this would not be fair to the others who didn't have this opportunity. Moreover, the only time I could make grade changes after the course had been completed, in compliance with university policy, was when there were clerical errors in grading or some unusual circumstance beyond the student's control.

Although it was generally pre-meds who came for grade changes, there were some unusual cases of interest. One was the young lady with whom I had never spoken before the course ended. Completely covered by a burka, only her sad dark eyes could be seen peering out at me in desperation. She had failed the course with one of the lowest grades and was deeply upset. As an exchange student from Dubai of the United Arab Emirates, she informed me that she needed at least a C in every course to remain in the U.S. "What can I do to pass your course?" she asked with tears pouring out of her eyes. "If I don't pass, they'll send me back to Dubai."With her grades, there was no way she could have spent even one hour per week studying. Trying my best to sound sympathetic, I told her it was now too late to do anything about her failing grade."

This may sound cruel, or at least hard-hearted, but what could I do? For a change I didn't mind following the university policy of not making grade changes. It is necessary to do some studying in order to pass my course, even without a curve. Begging for mercy is not sufficient in the court of academia.

9.

PRE-MEDS AND STRESS

Throughout the course of these stories, I may have seemed rather critical of pre-meds. In fact, I have great compassion for them as a general rule, and have mentored and befriended many. It must be extremely difficult for them to manage their lives when the competition for acceptance into medical school is so keen. So much depends on grades and that one MCAT exam that it is no wonder they often appear to act so poorly at times when other stressful situations occur. I have known many students who almost dropped out of school when faced with being dumped by a girlfriend or boyfriend. But some, like the twins, Ben and Ken, managed to handle the stress successfully by falling back on other activities, such as surfing in their case (see section 10). I will now describe a few others whom I mentored and whose passion for activities outside of science and medicine played a significant role in their alleviating stress and becoming successful doctors.

Ever since childhood, I have had great respect for medical doctors, possibly because I saw this profession as having attained the highest level of academic achievement. That is why, while mentoring some pre-meds who knew little about topics unrelated to Biology, I did my best to open their eyes, at least to the worlds of music, theater, literature, and sports. Often, these were "first generation college students," those whose parents had never completed American universities. They were generally very appreciative of this effort on my part, realizing that it would look very bad if, during an interview for medical school, they had never heard of people such as Johannes Brahms, George Bernard Shaw, or Babe Ruth. My mentees would come to my home for an evening of "cultural awareness" and dessert, and I always enjoyed it as much as they did, often learning more than I taught. After all, I knew little about their cultures, too.

Jarom was one of my star pupils and all-time favorite mentees. We first met while he was in my Introductory Biology course because he accepted my open invitation to play tennis. Jarom was in his sophomore year and already a member of the varsity team. Nevertheless, he always took it easy on me and was an outstanding coach. We became good friends during his remaining three years, and he still remains in touch after having completed a PhD/MD program. Right from the time of our first meeting, I couldn't believe how little this native Californian knew about the arts and literature. But what a thirst for knowledge he displayed! It was really impressive how he would take the little he learned from me and dive into much more depth about the subjects. At first a shy kid who hardly said a word, he soon became a young man who couldn't tell me enough about what he had learned. Tennis remained a favorite activity for Jarom, but it was no longer his only love. Learning became his main passion, and his breadth of knowledge was very impressive, as was his compassion. By the time he graduated, Jarom was most certainly the type of person I would like as my personal physician.

Another remarkable pre-med was Miriam. As a member of the Baha'i faith, Miriam's life was in grave danger, and she was forced to flee Iran shortly after Khomeini came into power. Speaking hardly any English, she attended community college and worked full time for several years before enrolling at UCSD. Throughout all her years as a college student, she received nothing but straight A's. Miriam served as a TA for me several times and was outstanding. Before leaving for medical school, she presented me with a beautiful gift of a poem by Hafiz, a famous 14th century Persian mystic philosopher, written in Farsi calligraphy by Miriam. His poems are reputed to have a beautiful musical quality, as well as a spiritual eloquence. I then learned that it was the study of Hafiz as well as calligraphy that helped Miriam reduce the great stress in her life. She is now a medical doctor with a family living in Los Angeles.

Music is a common activity for many scientists and medical doctors, but few take it as far as Annie did. This young lady graduated from Julliard in New York with a degree in music performance. She then decided that being a concert pianist was not sufficiently satisfying, and so she came to UCSD as a pre-med. She needed a full two years of further study in the sciences before she could even take the MCAT, all the time wondering whether she could do well in this completely different competitive field of study. Her stress was at least partially relieved by continuing to play the piano, sometimes together with amateur musicians such as myself. In retrospect, I think my violin playing may have done more to add to her stress, but she was always kind enough not to complain about it. Annie became very interested in homeopathy and went on to receive a doctorate in Naturopathy from Bastyr University, a pioneer institution in the field of natural healing.

From these few examples, it should be apparent that many of my favorite students were pre-meds, and that I gained a great deal of pleasure and knowledge from my association with them. I find it disappointing that most of my science colleagues don't share this point of view. They tend to shun pre-meds as if they were a type of pestilence, or at least pests, thinking that they want nothing more than an A and a good letter of recommendation. While this is true in some cases, it is definitely not a general rule. Scientists especially should not be so hasty in jumping to conclusions, taking time to examine the "data" from each individual.

10.

FIRST IMPRESSIONS AND UNCONSCIOUS BIAS

"Where are you from?" I ask so often when meeting a student who appears to be Asian. When their reply is somewhere like San Francisco, my first reaction immediately suggests a hint of confusion, perhaps even a trace of disbelief. "I mean not where your parents live now. Where were you born?" Even then the answer is often the same as before. That's when the truth comes out that because of their physical appearance, I make the unwarranted assumption that they must have been born in some country in Asia. Unlike people from most other lands, the physical appearance of Asians leads to the first impression that they must not be Americans. With the growing prejudice toward Asian Americans that is developing in our universities throughout the nation, it is important to consider the significance of first impressions and the meaning of unconscious bias.

In his fascinating book, "Blink," Malcolm Gladwell makes the point that we humans should trust and rely on our first impressions much more often. This is because we have a region in the brain that is specifically designed for recognizing a variety of signals that are produced during first impressions, and this recognition ability has been strongly selected throughout the course of evolution. A well known ability of this type is called the "fight or flight response." When suddenly a lion appears in your path, making this decision correctly can be a matter of life and death.

Making correct judgments of people in a fairly short time is not one of my strong points, however. I have often hired people, even after extensive interviews, only to discover later that they were entirely unsuited for the job. Perhaps I would have had better luck if I had trusted my first impression, but I doubt it. I probably have too many unconscious biases, as evidenced by the following story.

On a bright summer morning, I was walking across the quad on the way to my first lecture. Heading in the same direction were two guys, identically dressed in beach attire and both with long golden brown dreadlocks. My first thought, I'm ashamed to admit, was, "I hope they're not in my class. They should be out surfing from the looks of them." To my dismay, they headed straight into my classroom.

Thankfully, I didn't rely on my first impressions for long. Identical twins, Ben and Ken, turned out to be excellent students, and we soon developed what turned into a long lasting friendship. This was their very first college course, and it led to their selecting Biology for a major. They were not at all embarrassed to admit that they came to San Diego primarily because of its proximity to the beach. They were both highly ranked surfers and wanted to continue surfing while in college. I lost no time enlisting them as surfing instructors for my youngest son, Danny. We also enjoyed lots of tennis and lengthy discussions during their years at UCSD.

My negative feeling about surfers was completely dispelled by these twins. One evening en route to a coffee shop in La Jolla, Ken stopped in at the Hard Rock Café to speak to the manager. In less than a minute, Ken was being led to the bar with me close behind. "Give them anything they want all night," the manager instructed the bartender. Shocked, I asked Ken what was happening and was told to look up at the ceiling. Hanging there was a surfboard with Ken's autograph. Apparently, he had done a TV interview recently and was offered bar privileges in exchange. I was enjoying the company of a celebrity.

I have never surfed in my life, except for the Web, but thanks to the twins my name appeared in Surfer Magazine.

Ben and Ken were among the first professional surfers to attend medical school. In their interview for Surfer Magazine, they mentioned how I had been the main source of inspiration for them to do this, and that's what appeared in the article. They have now completed medical school and are well on their ways to a completely different type of successful career.

As for me, I will never trust my first impressions despite what it says in "Blink." I still wonder what it was about the twins' appearance that caused me to hope they would not be in my class. Apparently I had an unconscious bias toward surfers for some reason. I had never known any personally, nor had I ever had any interaction with a surfer. Yet despite this, within a few years after the birth of my first son, we sold our home near the beach in Bird Rock and moved to University City, about five miles inland from the beach. The main reason for this was that we did not want our children growing up too close to the ocean and becoming surfers. Coincidentally, this very same son is now an authority on the subject of unconscious bias. No, he is not a surfer, nor are any of his siblings. My bad!

11.

SEXISM

One specific and common type of politically incorrect behavior involves sexism. By definition, sexism entails discriminatory or abusive behavior towards members of the opposite gender, most often the female. It also includes the cultural attitudes and stereotypes that promote this behavior. From the time I joined the faculty in 1963, and throughout the '60's, only about 10% of the graduate students in the natural sciences were women. Most of my colleagues in Biology felt then that it was pointless to accept women to our program because they would get married and not have productive careers. Thankfully this clearly sexist viewpoint has disappeared, but as the following stories reveal, sexism is not always so obvious or well understood.

Almost every year I was fortunate to find tennis partners from among my many TAs and students. In need of a replacement for one of the three TAs who was ill, I announced at the start of class that I needed a fourth for doubles. To my surprise, not one hand was raised. I only waited a few seconds before noticing another of my TAs, Sharon, sitting in the second row. This triggered me to remember that she had several times asked to play tennis with me. Without a moment's hesitation, I announced "That's OK, Sharon will be my partner…and we'll win for sure because Naren and Barry will be looking at her instead of the ball." This brought down the house. Perhaps because Sharon was such a pretty TA, always well dressed and meticulously made up, most of the 300 students knew who she was and thought my comment was very funny. Admittedly, so did I.

To my surprise and dismay, Sharon did not. At the end of class, she came up to me in tears. She was terribly upset that I had said such a thing to the entire class. I couldn't imagine what I had said that offended her. She was pretty and she knew it, and so did everyone else. What was the problem? Sharon explained that I had "objectified her" by my statement, referring specifically to her looks and not her brains. Amazed that my joke had been taken as a sexist comment, I set up an appointment with her to discuss the matter after she had time to calm down. I totally expected a sexual harassment charge to be served even though I had been her mentor and close confidante for nearly three years.

A few months before this incident occurred, Sharon had broken up with her boy friend, Amir, whom I had also mentored. They had gone together for three years, and everyone saw them as an ideal couple destined for marriage. The summer after Amir graduated, they had traveled in Europe and had a wonderful time. In the fall, he started medical school 500 miles away. In less than two weeks after that, Sharon received the breakup letter…by email. Shocked, she came to me in tears to pour out her heart and soul. Besides providing an ear and a shoulder, I offered some useful counsel. I told her that she had two alternative paths. She could stay depressed for a long time, screw up her grades, and use this as an excuse for not getting accepted into medical school that year. Or she could tough it out and prove that she was indeed capable of reaching her goals in life. I was delighted that Sharon chose to tough it out. She did very well in her courses and her MCAT, and was accepted by several excellent medical schools.

When Sharon arrived for our appointment, she once again explained her feelings, but this time calmly. I told her that I was sorry I had referred to her good looks in front of the class, and that I now realized this was inappropriate. However, I added that my remarks were nothing compared with what she would face in the medical profession. She should try to develop a thicker skin and not let such matters bother her so much. Perhaps because I said I was sorry, her apology instead of a harassment charge arrived by mail soon thereafter. Sharon met a much nicer guy before graduating that year and is now married to him. I happily attended their wedding party.

Another charge of being a sexist came about as a result of a play I wrote, "Academic Matters." It is about an academic biologist, Prof. Joe Lehrer, who is on the verge of a cure for cancer. Unfortunately, Joe's social skills are poor, and he has great difficulty relating to his graduate student, Jil, his departmental chairman, Prof. Savanti, and a colleague, Prof. Ann Gates. Savanti is a male chauvinist pig of the first order, present in large part for comic relief. Joe may also have some leanings in that direction as he believes Ann's success as a scientist is more a result of her good looks than her brains. Jil uses her brains, hard work, and feminine charm as best she can to get ahead in what is generally considered a man's world, namely, academic science. One of the main themes of the play is to show that social interactions are very important in academic science, just as they are in every other endeavor.

My play was given two stage readings as part of the Revelle College 40th anniversary, with undergraduates playing all the roles. The audience of approximately 200 included students, faculty, and the community. I was delighted with the glowing reviews, as well as the fact that I at least heard nothing negative from anyone. Prof. Milton Saier commented that he "saw his life unfolding before his eyes." Not one person said a word to me about the play expressing sexism.

One aspect of the Hughes Scholars Program (HSP) which I directed involved outreach to several local high schools and community colleges. Our objective was to increase the attendance of under-represented minority students at UCSD in the area of the biological sciences. Carla, our Program Coordinator, worked with high school Biology teachers in developing a variety of after school programs for their students. After gaining approval from one of the teachers, I suggested to Carla that she read my play and tell me whether she liked the idea of selecting one or two scenes as a starting point for a discussion of what the life of an academic biologist entails. I thought the students would enjoy doing a little acting as a prelude to their discussion.

I never heard back from Carla. Instead, my supervisor, Asst. Vice Chancellor Loren Thompson, informed me that Carla had told him that she intended to file a charge of sexual harassment against me. Needless to say, I was shocked. I tried to talk with Carla about this, but she refused to discuss the matter. Her intentions were set. I tried telling her that the views of the characters did not necessarily reflect those of the author, but was met with silence. Dr. Thompson refused to talk with Carla for fear of getting embroiled in a law suit. Totally at a loss, I asked her whether she also planned to sue Shakespeare, but this too produced no response.

To my great relief, the Office of Sexual Harassment told Carla she had no case. I had not harassed her in any way, sexually or otherwise. Nevertheless, as a supervisor, I was required to take a thorough course on sexual harassment.

Unfortunately, this incident was the beginning of the end of HSP. There was no way I could continue working with Carla, and so I resigned as director. The grant from the Howard Hughes Medical Institute was not renewed. A wonderful program died, at least in part because of a misunderstanding of the meaning of sexism, but mainly due to an attempt to exploit it beyond reason.

Sexist attitudes still exist everywhere, even in the laboratories of the most prestigious universities, and they need to be confronted. Running away from them is of no use, nor is crying wolf when it is only a playwright pointing out these attitudes. Should we remove G.B. Shaw from our library shelves because of his belief that "Marriage occurs when two fools meet and make the same mistake at the same time"?

12.

POLITICAL CORRECTNESS

There are many times when you say exactly what you mean, or try to be as helpful as possible, but it is taken the wrong way. In this age of extreme political correctness, such times can lead to serious difficulties, such as law suits, or worse. A movie that illustrates this lesson very well is David Mamet's "Oleanna." In this story, a professor's career and home life are thoroughly ruined by a female student he is trying to help, not only because he failed in his efforts, but also for failing to handle the matter in a politically correct manner. There is far too much emphasis on the need for political correctness in our society today.

Shortly after accepting the position of Director of the Hughes Scholars Program, I was standing by the Mandeville coffee shop with my friend and supervisor, Dr. Loren Thompson. Loren was Assistant Vice Chancellor of Student Affairs, and he was telling me how hard it is to avoid sexual harassment charges from students and employees nowadays. He warned me that being an administrator was quite different than being a professor, and that I would have to be much more careful in my new position. Just looking at someone the wrong way or saying the wrong thing could lead to a problem, but "whatever you do, don't touch anyone," he advised. At precisely that moment, Cynthia came running over to me with her usual big smile and "Hi, Dr. Green," and threw her arms around me in a warm embrace. I stood there with both arms held stiffly at my side, looking at Loren over the shoulder of this tall, beautiful African American student, and pretended to be very uncomfortable. Finally I said to him, "Now what should I do?" He cracked up laughing as my point was quite obvious.

When I was first offered the position of Director of Academic Enrichment Programs (AEP) by Vice Chancellor Joseph Watson, I expressed my concern that it might not be appropriate for a Caucasian to be in the position of serving as the head of programs aimed at helping under-represented students. An African-American himself, Dr. Watson said not to worry, "it is the thoughts and deeds that count, not the color of one's skin." Joe served many years as a respected leader on the campus, and he certainly had my respect and admiration. On many occasions he was able to deal with touchy issues concerning minorities in a manner that would have proved much more difficult for someone with less integrity... and a white skin.

Without any thoughts or deeds, I soon managed to offend my African-American secretary. Situated in our new office quarters, this secretary had the computer that received all departmental messages, as well as my personal e-mails. Angie printed out all my messages and delivered them to me twice a day. I knew something was wrong one morning the moment Angie appeared, her eyes ablaze as she shoved the papers at me. "How dare you receive a joke like this, and from your son no less!" I took the papers calmly and read the joke. It concerned how one could tell that Jesus was black. It was definitely a racist type of joke, but at least to my way of thinking, it was not meant to be hurtful. I felt that Angie was over-reacting, intent on finding an excuse to get me in trouble, and that this e-mail would serve her purpose. I told her that I would deal with my son, but could not prevent everyone in the world from sending me jokes. Meanwhile, she should stop reading my mail.

I showed the joke to Dr. Watson's two African-American secretaries, both of whom thought it was very funny and not at all offensive. There is a fine line at times between a person being offended with reason and being offended due to over-sensitivity. In this case, I was found not guilty.

I could not be held responsible for someone else's political incorrectness, even if they were related to me.

I am often warned by my wife and close friends that my amiable attitude toward students is going to get me into serious trouble some day. But it makes me feel good when my TAs give me a hug at the start of a new quarter in front of my class of 350 students. And I like meeting my students and TAs for lunch and coffee, knowing that they must derive some pleasure from this interaction, too. Whether they call me Professor or Dr. Green or Mel, I treat them always as an equal. I know they care about me as a person they can trust and learn from, or they wouldn't bother inviting me. So if I can't be free to be me, I don't want to be, and to hell with PC.

13.

DRAWING ATTENTION

Natural beauty was not Kirstin's only attribute. She was also very intelligent, an excellent student, and quite athletic. Running over 20 miles every week kept her in great physical and mental condition. Without a doubt, Kirstin ranks as one of my most popular TAs of all time. I would often receive emails asking where her section met and whether it was too late to join it. Students also asked for her personal contact information, which I of course kept to myself. Dating students was forbidden to TAs as well as professors. Why she needed to wear that conspicuous tongue ring is still beyond me, but I certainly never had the nerve to ask. Kirstin always sat in the front row of my lectures with a perpetual smile that showed off her good looks as well as that ring. It took a lot of discipline for me to look elsewhere.

As with most of my TAs, I served as a mentor to Kirstin during the two years she served as my TA. She never discussed anything about her personal life with me, keeping our conversations strictly to academic matters. I assumed that with her good looks and personality, she never experienced a social problem. When she told me that she was going to put off applying to medical school until the year after her graduation, I questioned her reasoning. For me, the shortest route to any goal is always best unless there are some extenuating circumstances. Kirstin was under the impression that she could not apply to medical school until after taking the MCAT. Because she was planning to take this exam in August, she thought it would not be permitted to apply until after the exam was graded, some six weeks later. Since it is best to apply as early as possible, which means in June, this would cause her to miss an entire year. For most students, taking a year off is a fine idea as it gives them a chance to improve their qualifications in a variety of ways. But Kirstin had no special plans for what she would do that year after graduation, and she actually preferred not to delay attending medical school if it were at all possible. With my advice and encouragement, she did apply before taking the MCAT and was accepted.

Kirstin's parents were very grateful to me for this advice, probably because it saved them a year of considerable useless expense, and possibly because they suspected that Kirstin may have gotten involved with someone during her year of total freedom and changed her mind about going to medical school. As a reward, they invited my wife and me to a dinner celebration following their daughter's graduation. Driving to the restaurant, all I could think of was that tongue ring and what I might say about it. My wife assured me the subject would never arise, so I shouldn't worry about it, but I feared that, as usual, I would put my foot in it and say something totally inappropriate. She laughed and said my foot wouldn't fit into that ring. I have a knack for using precisely the wrong sayings.

It was a small informal dinner party, mostly friends of Kirstin's, and I was placed next to her father. No sooner was I seated and introduced when he confronted me with my worst fears. "So, Dr. Green, what do you think of Kirstin's tongue ring?" Taken aback, but almost never for a loss of words, I replied, "I hope she can remove it for her patients." Apparently her father was "into" that tongue ring as much as I. Now that Kirstin is a medical doctor, I wonder what she does to draw attention. Somehow I doubt that it's with a tongue ring.

Even in a room filled with 350 jean-clad, gene-learning students, one young man stood out from all the rest. Attired every day in a dark blue or black pin-stripe suit with vest and tie, Vicente looked like he had stepped out of a men's fashion magazine. Always seated in one of the first two rows, it was impossible not to fix my gaze on him often throughout my lecture. His appearance definitely attracted quite a bit of attention, not only from me, but also his classmates.

It wasn't long before Vicente approached me after lecture with an invitation to meet for coffee on campus. I looked forward to getting to know this character and finding out the reason for his formal dress. Not only his attire, but also his deep penetrating gaze and serious manner made it seem like Vicente was considerably older than his otherwise youthful appearance.

As with most of my students, Vicente insisted on paying for our coffees. However, in this case it was made evident that his wallet was stuffed with rather large bills. Our conversation revolved primarily around Vicente's life. He owned his own home in prestigious La Jolla, and it was large enough to house several of his friends, including a girl friend, whom he referred to as his monkey. He had a part-time job as a dress designer, a job that evidently paid quite well and kept him interested in the latest fashions. His only reason for taking my Biology course was to satisfy a Revelle College science requirement. I couldn't help but become suspicious that this guy was in some way connected with the Mexican equivalent of the Mafia. My curiosity about him soared.

As the academic quarter progressed, coffees evolved into lunches, dinners, and even invitations to parties at his home. Vicente always insisted on footing the bill. My curiosity was sufficiently aroused that I accepted several of these invitations, wondering what the real reason behind them could be. Was it merely the usual letter of recommendation, or was there some other motive?

Finally, at one of our lunches, Vicente confided that at the young age of 22, he was a severe diabetic, on the waiting list for a kidney transplant. That explained several questions I had about him, such as his handicapped license plate while seeming perfectly healthy. But I must confess that I remained skeptical of the validity of this story. It seemed possible, given his behavior, that Vicente used this story to gain certain campus privileges, such as the parking permit and extra time on exams granted by the Office of Disabilities.

When Vicente told me that he was "having some problems with the Revelle Provost Office," my suspicions seemed confirmed. Apparently he had dropped out of several classes in which he was failing, and now had insufficient credits to maintain his financial support from the university. He wanted me to write a letter of support to the Provost. But I couldn't imagine why this wealthy young man could possibly need financial support, and he never gave me any indication of actually being unhealthy. I made up a lame excuse that I didn't know what I could write that would be of any assistance.

That was the last time I heard from Vicente for nearly a year. Then I received a letter from one of his friends informing me that Vicente had almost died and was in the hospital receiving a new kidney. He wanted me to write to him. I was so sad, both from this news and also from having been so mistrustful. I had been totally misled by Vicente's impressive appearance and behavior, which evoked a type of reverse discrimination. No doubt beautiful and/or well-off people such as Marilyn Monroe have to overcome false impressions and biases, both conscious and unconscious, on a regular basis.

14.

CONNECTIONS

One criticism I have of UCSD, which is probably relevant to most research oriented universities, is that very few of the faculty serve as mentors for the undergraduates other than when they are engaged in research projects. This activity usually does not occur until the student's third or fourth year. Students whose parents have not completed an American university education, the so-called "first generation college students," are among those in greatest need of a faculty mentor during their first year on campus.

They tend to think that doing well in course work is the entire challenge and goal of their education, but they fail to realize that the university has far more to offer with regard to a student's overall development. They need advice from faculty mentors as well as staff counselors about the many facets of the university beyond the classroom, and the help necessary for them to make the important connections that will aid in achieving their dreams. I am convinced that who you know is often more important than what you know.

It grieves me no end when a student tells me that I am the only professor he has been able to talk with during his four years on campus. In an effort to get more faculty involved with students, I created a program called FSSI, the Faculty Student Staff Interaction Program. It soon became a student organization with about 25 members, with me as the faculty advisor. We would meet every Friday at the International Center for lunch. One or two students would bring a faculty or staff member as a guest, and during lunch the students would conduct an informal interview of the guest. For a change, the students were able to witness their instructors and administrators as actual human beings, even having lives outside of the university.

We were discussing whom to invite for the following week when Vera, a Freshman Biology major, suggested Kary Mullis. She didn't say Dr. Mullis, but instead used his first name, as if she actually knew him. Heads turned and eyes opened wide because several students knew that this man was a recent Nobel laureate. Mullis had discovered PCR, or

Polymerase Chain Reaction, the method used for amplifying a single molecule of DNA billions of times, thereby making it an extremely useful technology. For example, a single cell found at the scene of a crime could provide sufficient DNA for PCR to make it possible to identify the criminal. Paternity cases were another common example where this technology offered important application. I stated without hesitation that Dr. Mullis would be impossible to get as a guest for our little program. He was not even a member of our faculty, but had moved to La Jolla in semi-retirement because he liked surfing.

I was showing off a little with that tidbit of knowledge about Mullis. I had heard about him from a friend of mine, but had never met him. Vera, as it turned out, knew far more about him, and from a very reliable source…herself. At the young age of 18, she had interviewed him for the school newspaper. Evidently this mid-50's genius had found something attractive about this gorgeous blond, and after a few nights on the town, asked her to move in with him. There must have been something appealing about him, too, perhaps his fame and money for starters, so she accepted this "proposal." Attending banquets and conferences enabled Vera to meet many famous people, thus greatly promoting her opportunities to do some interesting feature stories for the paper. The FSSI students also received the benefit of Vera's connections by having Dr. Mullis join them for lunch. Vera was one of those rare and fortunate people who did not need anyone's help in making important connections.

A few years later, Vera invited me to her wedding. Not surprisingly, the groom was not Kary Mullis, nor was he present. But to my great shock, Vera's father did mention him in his speech after the ceremony. He seemed so proud of his daughter for having managed to make such "close contact" with this famous person. I don't think anyone else there thought this was so wonderful to bring up, especially not at this time. Connections are without doubt very important, but so is discretion. Fortunately, the groom was a very understanding young man.

15.

SHYNESS

We often say someone is shy without really having a good definition or understanding of the meaning of the word. The person we call shy may be reticent or speak quietly, or perhaps for one of many reasons, they don't interact readily with people, one on one and/or in a group. But there are also those who exhibit one or more of these behavioral traits for reasons other than shyness. In some cases, shyness is a serious condition that can lead to poor performance in school or at work, to clinical depression, and in extreme cases, even to suicide.

A case in point is the Asian-American student who graduated Revelle College with straight A's and was invited to present the keynote speech at commencement. Tony spoke about the excellent academic environment at UCSD, mentioning several of his professors by name and giving them credit for his outstanding performance and desire to learn. Then, he suddenly stopped speaking for several minutes. Tears welled up in his eyes and he became choked with emotion. When he regained his composure, he told the audience that he had never in his life gone out on a date, and that he would trade all his A's for just one date. Tony had been too shy to ask a girl out, and he deeply regretted it. But not every shy person copes with life as well as Tony.

Before the age of 10, my daughter Jessica was anything but shy. Growing up in the midst of three older brothers, she was used to being the center of attention. My beloved daughter was six years young the first time she visited my Biology class. I was up on a stage lecturing in the new auditorium used for showing movies, and there were 350 students sitting in the plush seats, trying to take notes in the dark and stay awake. It was the day fathers brought their children to work and showed them what they did for a living.

Jessica was sitting with her mother in the very back row when I announced to the class that my daughter was present and wanted to say a few words. She knew this was coming, and without hesitation marched down the aisle and up on stage, confidently took the microphone in her tiny hand, and looked out at the huge audience. "I forgot what I was going to say," was all she said, but that was enough. The audience burst into laughter and applause, and Jessica departed from my classroom until the following year. Unfazed by her lapse in memory the previous year, she announced loud and clear, "You better not fall asleep in my Daddy's class or he'll be mad at you!" Again she received a rousing ovation. The next year she amazed me and the entire class by asking them a question. "What kills more, animals or plants?" They were stunned and didn't respond. After a long silence, Jessica, age 8, informed the college students, "Plants kill more. Think about weeds killing other plants around them." They were definitely impressed with this young, self-confident teacher.

But something changed Jessica, and by the age of 12 she started behaving as if she were painfully shy. Webster defines shyness as being "bashful, retiring, and timid," and Jessie was all of these with everyone other than her immediate family. Her life at school had become a torture, and we parents grew quite concerned. Her mother, Lynn, worked at the same private school Jessie attended, so she was able to observe the situation first-hand. Jessie's former friends, the five other girls in her small 6th grade class, for unknown reasons had turned against her. When they saw her approaching, they would withdraw and whisper secrets to one another. Who can imagine what they said, but that didn't matter. Jessie had been ostracized from the group, and she understandably felt terrible. Lynn shared her daughter's feelings when she saw her sitting alone every day during recess while the other students were having fun together. This reminded Lynn all too clearly of her own shyness, especially at Adelphi University, where, far from her family in Ecuador, she had felt miserably shy and lonely for two years. To this day she still has nightmares about being at that school.

When Jessica began the 7th grade, I had the bright idea of introducing her to one of my TAs. Candice was a very friendly, outgoing young lady, and like Jessica, she was very much into art. I thought that by having a college student as a friend, Jessica might gain some self-confidence and revert to her former vivacious personality. Candice was very receptive to this idea, and she tried her best to help. She taught my daughter how to do oil paintings, and despite the considerable age difference, they actually became good friends. But this experiment had a very limited range of success. Although Jessie's demeanor away from school improved somewhat, she still wasn't accepted by "the group" at school, so her behavior there remained unchanged. She gave the impression of being too shy to integrate into her former circle of friends, and she was clearly miserable. Despite all the successful counseling I had done with my students at the university, I felt like a total failure with my daughter.

Before the academic year ended, Lynn and I decided that Jessica should transfer to a public school at the start of 8th grade. However, we feared that shyness may have become a permanent personality trait in our daughter, and we worried that she would continue finding life difficult and remain terribly unhappy. Fortunately this was not the case. During the orientation session, Jessie quickly made two girl friends, and they remained good friends throughout her school years. Her extreme shyness and depressed demeanor disappeared in a very short time, and our formerly delightful, vivacious daughter reappeared as if by magic. She enjoyed school once again and soon became popular and involved in extra-curricular activities. I began to wonder whether Jessie's previous problem actually had anything to do with shyness.

I have known many students who appeared "shy as a church mouse," whatever this old saying means. One I mentored for an entire year without her ever looking me in the eye. Ying only spoke when I asked her a question, and then in a voice so soft I had difficulty hearing her. She was an excellent student and aspired to become a doctor. I worried that she would never do well enough in an interview to be accepted into medical school. But Ying was only in her Freshman year, and often students like her change so much by their Junior year that they are hardly recognizable. At times it is simply a matter of gaining maturity, or becoming more at ease with English as their second language, or adapting to their new environment. Parents and teachers must realize that even extreme shyness can be overcome under the right circumstances. It is definitely not an irreversible trait. However, finding the right solution to the problem is not so easy.

I think it likely that we are too quick to judge a person as being shy. There are so many reasons for behaving in ways that create the impression of shyness without actually having a shy personality. For example, in some cultures, looking an elder in the eye is considered rude, as is smiling without covering one's mouth. One unforgettable class I attended focused on learning to cope with being single again after a divorce. There were close to a hundred participants in it, and it lasted five weeks. In the last session, the instructor asked for a show of hands from all those who felt shy. When I raised my hand, several people looked at me and laughed boisterously. Clearly my self-perception did not match theirs. But I am certain that, at least in my teens, I was extremely shy... I think.

16.

SUCCESS

My eldest son, Sascha, was another member of the family who benefited a bit from my teaching experience. Being very shy from the outset, he would avoid other children at the playground and sit by himself all day at the Montessori pre-school. But this shyness didn't seem to affect his happiness nor his academic performance throughout his pre-college years, and he did well enough to be accepted into UCSD. Having his dad teaching at the same school must have posed some awkward problems, but there were also some advantages.

Toward the end of his sophomore year, still without having declared a major, Sascha approached me with a question: "What do you think about the idea of my being a pre-med student?" Without a moment's hesitation, I glibly replied, "Why not? Almost every other student here is a pre-med." Sascha had never before mentioned anything about wanting to become a doctor, and he was not one to make decisions quickly or early. To this day, he is always the last to select menu items. I have no idea what caused him to arrive at this idea, but I felt confident that he could become at least as good a doc as any of my other students.

In the fall quarter of his junior year, Sascha came to me with another question. He had room for one more course and wondered what to take. I told him that pre-meds often did some research for course credit and he agreed that was a good idea. Then I informed him this was the last week to sign up for research for the winter quarter, and that it was necessary to have the approval of a faculty sponsor before doing so. Of course he had no one in mind. As luck would have it, I happened to be in charge of this program for the Biology Department that year. After a brief discussion, I put Sascha in contact with Dr. Rick Lieber, who was in the Department of Orthopedics, and all the paper work was handled on time; i.e., within a few days past the deadline. This last minute decision turned out to be critical, as it led to an interesting research job that summer and an excellent letter of recommendation from Dr. Lieber to medical school.

My son Sascha came into closer contact with his Dad, the professor, when he took my course, The Molecular Basis of Disease, and again when he served as a TA for my Introductory Biology course. There were well over 350 students in the Disease course, mostly pre-meds. Rather than lecturing, I invited all the speakers, experts in their fields of biomedical research, to present their latest findings. I would introduce the speaker and look for Sascha in the audience. For the first two weeks, he was nowhere to be found. I grew so nervous thinking there was no way he could pass this course without attending lectures. Since there was no textbook, I prepared exams that were based entirely on the lectures. He would surely fail and not get into medical school. His life would be ruined.

Finally, he came to our home for dinner, and I could restrain myself no longer: "Why don't you attend the lectures in my course? How do you expect to pass it without even showing up?" Always in complete control, Sascha replied calmly, "Relax, Dad, I've been there every day. I have to come from across campus and I get there right after you introduce the speaker and sit down." That's when I realized teaching a son in your own class poses some serious problems.

Fortunately, having Sascha as my TA turned out to be a lot of fun. It was a summer course with only 35 students and 2 TAs. The TAs led class discussions after every one of my lectures. When Sascha stood in front of the class, we took turns poking fun at one another to the delight of the students. I complained to the students that because Sascha was so good looking, I was no longer getting any invitations to coffee. He only smiled, acknowledging the obvious. His shyness as a teen had long since disappeared and was replaced by great confidence.

Now that Sascha is a successful physician and professor at Harvard Medical School, I sometimes wonder how his shyness was replaced with the confidence required to achieve this position. I see so many shy students who could benefit from such knowledge. Did I teach him anything that helped in this transformation, or was it simply a matter of maturation? I asked him recently whether he felt I had ever taught him anything. His response was very gratifying. "The most important thing you taught me was that you must define success for yourself. Don't let anyone define it for you." I had always encouraged Sascha to choose his own path, and to my great joy, he did so and has succeeded admirably. I still have no idea how he overcame his shyness, or if he ever did.

Judging from surveys I have conducted, very few university students have defined success for themselves. Many of those surveyed were pre-meds, dutifully following paths laid out for them by one or both parents. Some have even completed medical school before realizing medicine is not for them. Then there are those who graduated with a major in Biology, and yet have worked for years in various non-scientifically related positions, such as waiting on tables, painting houses, and parking cars. As in Samuel Beckett's famous play, "Waiting for Godot," these lost souls seem to be waiting for someone (or something) to come along and tell them what to do with their lives. There are so many career choices possible today...some think too many. But isn't it better to have lots of choices than very few, or none?

17.

FOLLOW YOUR PASSION

I never knew a more focused person than Danny, my youngest of three sons. As with all of my children, Danny was offered music lessons at a young age, in his case piano at the age of five. But unlike the others, Danny possessed real talent. Parental pride made it difficult to determine whether this talent was exceptional, but I definitely thought it was. His teacher arranged for his first recital, together with her other students, at a neighbor's home. Each student performed a short piece lasting a few minutes, took a bow, and hastily left the piano. Danny played his piece, then continued on with another that had not been scheduled. He then started on with a third number. Somewhat embarrassed, I went to the piano and whispered that it was time to give another student a turn, but he paid no attention and kept on playing. I took hold of his right hand and pulled him from the piano while he continued playing with his left. This should have been enough to clue me in about his love for music, but at the time, I just thought it was funny.

A couple years later, Danny's teacher scheduled a more formal recital, this one with a printed program. On the day before this event, disaster struck our home. Danny's beloved pet rabbit, Harry, disappeared, leaving him heartbroken. His Mom and I were very sympathetic, and went so far as to permit him to skip his recital the next day. But Danny would have none of it. He went on stage and performed so beautifully that he was the only one to receive a rousing standing ovation. I was in tears, as was Lynn, but Danny was as cool as could be. It was clear that music came first in his life.

But kids change as they become teens, and as Danny approached the age of 13, he surprised me with his request to stop taking piano lessons. It was not because of his teacher or any other clear reason. With my love for music, you can imagine how shocked and sad I felt. What could I do to prevent what I considered a terrible mistake? By sheer good luck, I came up with the idea of buying Danny a keyboard and told him to just have fun making music with it. Little did I realize at the time the amazing things he would accomplish with this keyboard. For nearly two years, our home resounded with the music of Nirvana, and nothing else. Danny used his computer to record 60 of their songs, all arranged with four parts. In my "unbiased" opinion, they sounded far better than in the original version.

Next came two years of playing and recording nothing but Ska, all the while improving his technique without lessons. One evening Lynn and I took Danny to see a movie about the Buena Vista Social Club, a group of elderly, formerly famous Cuban jazz musicians. Ska disappeared from Danny's life the next day, and Latin jazz replaced it. I believe his ability to focus so completely on one thing at a time was largely responsible for the great improvement in his musicianship without lessons.

By now it was time to select a college and a major. To my great surprise, Danny decided to major in Chemistry while attending nearby UCSD. He had done well in Chemistry in high school, but he had never shown any particular enthusiasm for the subject. Nor did he at college. His dorm had a piano in the lounge, and Danny spent more time playing it than with all his classes combined. In less than six months, he switched his major to Music Performance and became much happier. He started taking piano lessons again, relearned how to read music, and to my great surprise, developed an interest in classical music and opera. He graduated as the first to receive Honors in Jazz Performance, and is currently recognized as one of the top jazz pianists and composers in San Diego.

Danny's burning passion for music as well as his talent has brought great joy to his listeners, and I am thrilled every time I hear him perform. Because I play the violin, people often ask whether Danny inherited his musical talent from me. Perhaps, but I doubt it. My ability starts and ends with reading the written notes and trying my best to play them in tune. Danny, on the other hand, never plays the same song twice the same. His special talent lies in his creative ability to improvise and compose new music. As I jokingly told his older brothers, both of whom are physicians, "anyone can become a doctor, but it takes a special gift to become a pianist and composer." It's not easy, but I try to keep those doctors humble.

Danny admitted to me recently that his only reason for choosing Chemistry as a major was because he thought this would please me. Even though I have always advised my students to define success for themselves and follow their passions when deciding on a career, somehow my own son did not get this message, and he almost made the terrible mistake of trying to please his father when choosing a major and a career. Fortunately, for reasons still not clear to me, Danny quickly discovered the folly in this decision and dropped Chemistry. I would like to think that perhaps he got my message after all, and just needed some time to gather the courage to follow his dreams and his passion.

18.

SLOW STARTERS

Not every smart youngster is a good student by any means, because good students must put up with the "system," paying attention to boring lectures, studying for all the exams, and doing all the tedious homework to get those A's. And let's not forget about class behavior, which also greatly influences how the teachers like you, at least in kindergarten through 12th grade, and what the teachers think about you factors into your grade a lot more than it should, sometimes even in college.

My second son, Ari, was clearly very bright and well liked, at least by his peers, but you wouldn't know it from his grades in junior and senior high school. For reasons perhaps only knowable through psychoanalysis, Ari never did any homework and rarely studied for an exam. On the basis of good test scores, he somehow managed to pass all his courses and graduate high school, but not with a high enough GPA for admission to a university. Ari was immersed in a "catch 22" situation: he had no particular goal in life, and without a goal, he was unmotivated and did poorly in school, which prevented him from getting into a good college and finding a goal. He took a variety of minimum wage jobs that enabled him to get by, living at first with his mother and later sharing an apartment with friends. He flipped hamburgers, copied keys, developed photos, bussed tables, and got involved in lots of mischievous activities with friends who were in much the same boat. There seemed to be no way to change this bright young man's path that was leading nowhere, and because this was my son, the pain in my heart cannot be overestimated. Having provided guidance to so many UCSD students, I nevertheless felt helpless with my own son.

While employed in all these menial jobs, Ari attended Mesa Community College off and on for five years. I advised him to take only one, or at most two, courses per semester that he thought might be enjoyable until he found a field that he really liked. Otherwise he would do no better than he had in high school, and this would lead to an accumulation of poor grades, making it hard, if not impossible, to get into a 4-year college later. Fortunately, he took this advice. After three years of exploration at Mesa with no evidence of any significant progress, a star finally appeared in Ari's dark skies and provided some light in his life. The star's name was Lauren, a serious student at San Diego State University who also happened to be very attractive. Soon after Lauren came into Ari's life, he and I started having some serious career discussions for the first time. I don't believe for a moment that this timing was merely coincidental. Ari was definitely determined to impress Lauren that he was serious about finding a meaningful career.

In about a year after this fortuitous romance began, Ari had accumulated enough course units and satisfactory grades to gain admission to SDSU. Because of his love for sports of all kinds, I advised him to major in Physical Education. This was a field I knew he could do well in, and I thought that he would make an excellent PE teacher. Young kids always loved Ari, and vice versa. Somewhat to my surprise, my son took his father's advice again even though he had no intention of becoming a teacher, having experienced more than enough of the school system. I had recently taken Ari to meet Dr. Frank Powell, an exercise physiologist at UCSD, and to my delight he became interested in learning more about this field. This fit in perfectly with kinesiology, which was one of the choices within a Physical Education major at SDSU. At last a pathway to a desirable goal had appeared, and Ari was more than ready for it.

With a goal in mind and a girl friend for motivation, Ari started getting A's instead of C's in most of his courses. It soon became time to apply for graduate school. For more than a year Ari had been planning on becoming a Physician Assistant (PA), but after completing the application for PA school, he stunned me with a question. "What do you think of my applying to become a Doctor of Osteopathy?" Ari and I had first heard of the DO degree very recently as a result of a program that I had created and was directing at UCSD, the Health Professions Program. Training for a DO was similar to that of an MD, but Ari had a better chance for admission to a DO school. Although good grades and a high score on an entrance exam were necessary for admission to both, I believed that recent records and an interest in holistic medicine were more important to the DO programs than one's overall academic performance, unlike the MD programs.

Now 25 years of age, Ari would be required to delay graduation from SDSU for an entire year so that he could take several required courses, including Organic Chemistry, Physics, and a few Biology courses. With a wedding planned to Lauren for that summer, this delay would create a major financial difficulty for the newlyweds. Nevertheless, with total support from Lauren, as well as my encouragement, Ari decided to aim high and go for the doctor's degree rather than becoming a PA. As I often said, you won't go higher in life than you aim.

That year even with such a heavy science course load, Ari also managed to work part time, volunteer with a DO, and study for the medical admissions exam...the dreaded MCAT. Many UCSD students spend full time for several months doing nothing but studying for the MCAT. Now highly motivated, Ari not only got straight A's in all the science courses, he did so well on the MCAT that the Kaplan Company hired him as an instructor in their medical test preparation program. He was admitted by all of the DO schools for which he applied, and is today a highly successful doctor of medicine with a specialty in pain management.

I often wonder what was responsible for Ari's eventual success. At the age of 21, I doubt whether anyone who knew him would have guessed that his becoming a doctor of any kind was at all possible. Despite his dislike for school, at least throughout high school, Ari spent 5 years at Mesa Community College, 3 years at SDSU, 4 years at Midwestern College of Osteopathy, and then another 4 years as an intern and resident. Obviously the finding of a motivational force, and a strong one like Lauren, played a major role in getting him on track. She would certainly not tolerate a guy with little ambition. Staying on track and becoming successful also required a great deal of patience, perseverance, and perspiration, the three P's to success. In addition, I'd like to think my own patience with Ari throughout his difficult years of maturation, as well as some guidance at critical moments, especially when he had to select a major at SDSU and make the decision about DO school, played some role in his ultimate success. But who knows? It is often more difficult for a parent than someone unrelated to play the role of mentor.

When I mentor students, Ari is my favorite example of a person who took a slow, non-linear path to reach his goal. Although a straight line is the shortest way to any destination, there are many other paths that can lead you there. In many cases, "the one less traveled by" may be the best, and even if not the best, it just may be the only one possible. This reminds me of a favorite saying of my high school Chemistry teacher, Mr. Lon Colborn: "We often learn more by beating around the bush than by jumping straight into the bushes." The circuitous path Ari took certainly taught him many lessons that will help him throughout his life.

19.

EARLY STARTERS

S ome people just seem to know what they want to become professionally from very early in their lives. More often, some fortuitous event or encounter at a later age provides the impetus that shapes one's career. It may be a teacher who takes a particular interest in a student, or an internship that leads to an exciting part-time job. In my counseling of Biology majors looking for some research experience, I found two extremes: those who knew very clearly what they wanted to do and were not interested in anything else, and those who thought they would like almost every type of biological research. It was relatively easy helping the narrowly focused ones find a research opportunity with a professor. However, if for some reason the student became unhappy in that lab, it often led to their looking for an entirely new direction in life. Those who liked everything had a hard time making up their minds about what research area to choose, but once having done so, they were generally pleased with the experience.

With the aim of keeping students engaged in the field of biology, my most difficult challenge was with the narrowly focused ones. These were quite often "early starters," becoming interested in biology and other fields of science at an early age and thinking they knew exactly what they wanted to do in their careers. For example, some were determined to make a major contribution to understanding the cause of cancer or to a better treatment for cancer. I tried to help them realize that there were many approaches to attacking a complex problem such as a disease like cancer, and that a variety of experiences in different labs would be most beneficial.

I began counseling large numbers of students as a result of two administrative positions: Director of Academic Enrichment Programs (AEP) from 1994-1999, and Director of the Hughes Scholars Program(HSP) from 2006-2009. AEP involved enhancing undergraduate educational experiences in every way imaginable. Under AEP was the Faculty Mentor Program, which helped students with all majors find a faculty member to sponsor their research. The main objective of HSP was to increase the number of underrepresented minority students who completed their degrees in the biological sciences. We established an outreach program for middle school and high school students, as well as providing assistance for those already at UCSD. I consider any student interested in science before entering college an "early starter." At that age, all I cared about was sports, and it still amazes me that I ever became a scientist as I had virtually no encouragement in this direction before entering graduate school.

Tram was one of those students who wanted to become a medical doctor from childhood. Born in Hanoi, Vietnam, she came to America with her parents at the age of 12. Her father had been a doctor before fleeing Vietnam, but he had a difficult time learning English and never was able to continue practicing medicine in the States. As with so many immigrants, he worked hard at jobs far beneath his former status in order to provide the best opportunities for his children. He made it clear to Tram that it was his fervent wish for her to become a doctor, and she felt it her duty to honor that wish.

I met Tram during her sophomore year when she became a member of HSP. Since neither parent graduated from an American university and the family income was low, she qualified for this program. She was enrolled in a seminar course I offered called "Strategies for Success in Science." Meeting once per week for an hour, it provided the opportunity to listen to professors talk about their careers in the biological and medical fields. The students were also given advice on how to talk to professors, not only about the courses they were taking, but also about all sorts of things that might be personally beneficial, such as research opportunities and letters of recommendation.

One of my class sessions dealt directly with the topic of success. I told the students that it was essential to define success for themselves before someone else, such as a parent or teacher, defined it for them. We took time in class to write our definitions of success and then discuss them. Most of the students had never actually thought about this before, at least not consciously. Their definitions covered a wide range, from achieving fame and wealth to getting married and enjoying life with their family. One very unusual idea was that being able to enjoy a good night's sleep would be sufficient to constitute success for that belabored student, especially if it occurred on a regular basis.

After our last session ended, Tram approached me and began to cry before saying a word. After composing herself, she told me that as a result of this seminar course, she now had the strength to tell her father that she really did not want to become a doctor. She had come to realize that her true love was English literature, and that she wanted to be a teacher. Her childhood dream was in actuality her father's dream, not hers. I considered the seminar a major success for Tram.

John was another "early starter" who knew precisely from his senior year in high school what he wanted to do with his life. In his third year at UCSD, John joined the Faculty Mentor Program and came to me for help in finding a research professor. Unlike almost all the other students in this program, John had a definite idea of the research he wanted to conduct. He just needed someone who would provide the facilities for him to carry out that research. It is the rare professor who will do this because their grants specify rather clearly what has to be done. However, if the grants are large enough, and if the prof is sufficiently tolerant of someone else's idea being tested, usually when it fits in with his own ideas, there is a chance this can happen.

I was opposed to John's plan from the start. He had learned in high school that cancer cells grow better than normal cells in an anaerobic (oxygen free) environment. This is because tumors often develop before there is a good source of blood, which supplies the oxygen via hemoglobin in the red blood cells to all cells in the body. Therefore, he reasoned that cancer cells grow primarily by a fermentative pathway, namely, glycolysis, which uses glucose as an energy source and does not require oxygen. This led John to the idea that supplying cells with lots of oxygen and no glucose should favor the growth of normal cells.

Not only did I disagree with his reasoning, I also told him that with his limited exposure to the laboratory, it would be preferable to get a more general training in a biochemistry laboratory before attacking such a complex problem as the cure of cancer. But John was adamant, so I found him a lab in which the prof would allow him to test his idea. In less than a month, John returned with a sullen expression. Both the normal cells and the cancer cells died when no glucose was present in their growth medium. He had not realized the well-known fact that growth in the presence of oxygen also demands sugar. Moreover, high oxygen accelerated the growth of both the normal and the cancer cells when glucose was present. His research advisor allowed him to learn all this by doing the experiments.

John was so disillusioned that he was ready to quit science altogether, but I convinced him to stick with his dream of curing cancer. After all, this had been my dream, too, and it helps to dream (see "Creativity and Courage"). It just wasn't such a simple matter. A lot of learning and experience would definitely be advantageous, and there were many possible approaches in addition to his metabolic attack. I mentioned gene therapy and immunotherapy among others, and sent him off with a few books to read. We met often after that, and John became more and more excited about becoming a cancer researcher.

Following graduation from UCSD, John earned an MD along with a PhD in Molecular Medicine. He got in on stem cell research from near the time of its inception. This is a field that had not even been heard of while John was an undergraduate. Soon he was publishing groundbreaking papers on the use of stem cells on cancer patients. Developing an open minded approach, along with the necessary hard work, was the key to John's success in science, enabling him to get past what might have caused his early start to become an early finish.

20.

"Older" Students
in Science

The love of science often occurs at a very young age. Some movie or lab demonstration or animal found wandering with a broken leg is enough to whet a curious child's appetite for a lifetime. But there are also those less common cases where an interest in science develops at a later stage of life. From my experience, those who have taken many years to find their path often have reasons of considerable variety and interest. The following stories are based on my interviews with community college students who were enrolled in a program I directed at UCSD, the Hughes Scholars Summer Research Program. This program was designed to assist underrepresented minorities and first generation low income students complete their majors in biologically related fields of science.

Ben is a young man you would not expect to find majoring in Biology. I met him at a beach party put on to welcome students in the summer research program. These included sixteen undergraduates and nine community college students. Ben immediately caught my attention, being very outgoing and friendly. He seemed more like a salesman than a scientist. As I learned more about him, the reasons for this soon became apparent.

Coming from Milwaukee, Wisconsin after a seven year absence from academic pursuits, Ben is clearly very happy being a student again. Now in his second year at Mesa Community College, Ben is planning to transfer to UCSD after one more semester. He intends to major in Molecular and Cellular Biology. By then he will be nearly thirty years of age. This summer he is doing research on diabetes in Dr. Kumar Sharma's lab at the Medical School. Although this is his very first experience with research, he already sees himself working on diabetes for the rest of his career. According to Ben, "Research is far more enjoyable than any science lab course."

"So why did it take seven years from the time you graduated high school until you began Mesa College?" I asked between tosses of a football. Ben confessed that he did very poorly his first semester of college right after high school. So poorly, in fact, that he dropped out and became an auto parts salesman for the next seven years. Content just with passing grades in high school, Ben had not developed the study skills and attitude needed for success in college. He was admittedly "lazy" even though he liked science and literature. His one semester in college resulted in a rude awakening to the fact that he could no longer get by without some serious effort, and he was not yet ready for that.

What brought Ben back to his early interest in science was mostly a matter of maturation rather than any specific influence. But it did require the courage of his convictions and the persuasion of a cousin/best friend to strike out on his own in California. Ben had dreamt of becoming a scientist from the age of twelve, having enjoyed many shows about Nature on PBS. So he gave up his lucrative job as a salesman, turning down the offer of a big raise, and aimed for a career in an unknown world he had heard of only from a few high school courses and TV shows.

Older and more experienced than most of his classmates, Ben has the utmost confidence in his ability to succeed. His study habits have improved greatly, primarily due, he thinks, to his ability to engage teachers with questions before leaving class in a state of confusion. Evidently he is putting his interpersonal communication skills to good use. Now, after only a few weeks of experience in laboratory research, Ben is definitely committed to a career in science and thrilled with this decision. He has me sold on his plans, too.

Britte arrived in Twenty-Nine Palms, California in December, 2003, shortly after marrying a U.S. Marine from Puerto Rico. Having spent her life in Colombia, S.A., Britte spoke very little English. She was raised by her mom, her father having left the family when she was very young. It was far from an easy life, and attending college after graduation from high school was not in the immediate picture because this was far too expensive. Instead, Britte worked in a clothing store for a few years, helping her mom pay the bills, then married and left her home for a new life.

As I have seen with many other students, one key life experience triggered Britte's initial interest in science. At the age of seven, she suffered an appendicitis attack with severe complications caused by peritonitis. For many months, this young girl could not play with her friends, having to rest at home. She wondered throughout her childhood how this illness was caused. Fascination with biomedicine had unobtrusively entered her consciousness at a very early age. While in high school, an even more painful event occurred: Britte's grandmother died of cancer. They had been very close, and this came as a terrible shock.

It was around this time that Britte discovered her mother's high school biology text books gathering dust on a shelf. For some reason, these books appealed to her more than any others, and she devoured them just for fun every day. Although discouraged from a career in science by her mother, a high school Chemistry teacher first put this idea into her head. The subject seemed "very exciting," and she loved "just seeing the chemicals and the laboratory equipment." She even very much enjoyed writing lab reports, something most Chemistry students despise.

Shortly after coming to California, Britte began studying English in college ESL courses. In 2005 she enrolled in Palomar Community College as a full time student. At first her lecture notes were taken in Spanish, then translated into English at night. Although time consuming, this really helped her learn the material. Once again, science and math were her favorite subjects. She did so well that she was accepted by UCSD for the winter quarter of 2009.

With one year to go before graduating with a major in Biology, Britte is happily engaged in a research program funded by the Hughes Scholars Program (HSP). Her husband doesn't mind this second engagement a bit, being quite supportive of her education and plans for a biomedical science career. Still motivated to make a contribution toward the treatment of cancer, Britte is doing research in the laboratory of Dr. Boris Minev in the UCSD Cancer Center. Minev's research is in the area of cancer immunotherapy.

Throughout my interviews with Britte, I wondered how this modest young woman was coping with the highly competitive pressures of a Biology major. Her immediate answer: "the Hughes Scholars Program. HSP made me feel more like at home." It is "like a window to see what opportunities are in science." Like J. D. Salinger's Seymour Glass in "The Catcher in the Rye," Britte sees through the window very clearly.

Norma came up to me after my third lecture in Biology 1, a deep sadness evident in her eyes. "Can I make an appointment to speak with you privately? I feel so lost." We met in my office the next day, not the coffee shop where I hold most of my "office hours." It was clear this meeting needed privacy.

Tall, blond, and very attractive, Norma's good looks were overshadowed by her obvious sadness. She must have felt very comfortable confiding in this elderly professor, because it took little time before her cause for despair came pouring out along with the tears. "I feel so old here. These kids are so smart, and I feel so dumb around them." Norma was the mother of three children, and this was her first year back in college after a ten year absence. All of twenty-eight years of age, she had borne her first child at the age of 18 while a college freshman. She was forced to drop out of school to get a job and raise her child. Two others came soon after, together with all the difficulties of raising her children as a single mother. It had been quite a struggle just to survive, but now a "sugar daddy" was helping finance her way back to college. I asked no questions about this relationship.

Norma's goal was a career in the health sciences, perhaps as a nurse or a medical technician. But her high school courses had long been forgotten, and everything seemed so different now. The worst thing, though, was that she felt "so old" around her classmates. I told her that the students who returned after many years of absence were generally my top students, not at first, but by the end of the course. They were the most serious about succeeding, so they studied very hard, and they weren't afraid to ask questions when they didn't understand something.

After that, Norma came to my office hours almost every week. From her questions, it was clear she had spent a lot of time studying, and her test scores reflected her efforts. I was not surprised when she ended up with one of the top grades in my course. We kept in touch throughout her years at UCSD, and I was delighted when she asked for a letter of recommendation to medical school. Her record at UCSD was excellent, and I was confident that Norma would become a highly successful doctor, one who truly cared about her patients.

Considering the many roads students have traversed to become scientists, can any conclusions or generalizations be made about what factors are most important in this decision? It's really hard to say, but one rather curious analogy does stand out in my mind. Becoming a scientist is like falling in love and getting married. At first there is the feeling of exciting infatuation, possibly triggered by a teacher or the subject material of a course or book. The excitement grows as more is learned and shared with others. As one advances from course work to the experience of actual research, infatuation develops into the deeper feeling of true love. This becomes all the more thrilling as discoveries are made while delving ever deeper into the hidden mysteries of Nature. When it becomes apparent that one cannot live without being a scientist, a sort of marriage has taken place between the captivated researcher and his love...Science. As with the married couple, the scientist is now ready to enjoy the fruit of his impassioned labors for the rest of his life. With Science, however, unlike so many marriages, divorce occurs very rarely.

21.

SCIENCE VS. RELIGION

I have advised quite a few Biology students who have a deep conflict about evolution as a result of their religious upbringing. In every one of my Introductory Biology courses, both for majors and non-majors, several students got up and left the classroom as soon as I mentioned that the lecture would be about evolution. One of the most troubled students I knew was Cynthia. An African-American with a very strong fundamentalist faith in Christ, she had great difficulty resolving what she had learned from her religious background with what she was expected to accept from her courses at UCSD. We had many lengthy discussions about this conflict and the whole dilemma of faith vs. scientific reasoning. One rather simplistic view I presented helped her get past this problem.

To evolve means to change, and there is no doubt that life on our planet is in a state of flux. Hundreds of species are disappearing every year, and it is obvious that mutations can lead to changes even overnight, as with bacteria and yeast cells in laboratory experiments. I told her that God could have designed change in his Divine plan for life on Earth. That is, the existence of evolution does not mean that God does not exist. She liked this idea, especially after hearing that even Einstein believed in a Creator of the universe. So many students think that being a scientist means that they cannot believe in God. I knew that this concept of evolution was against Fundamentalist Christian belief, but at least it seemed to help matters for Cynthia. She was able to complete her major in Biology, graduate with an excellent record as a pre-med and attend medical school.

The Creationists' and Intelligent Designers' attack on Darwinian evolution is quite different from that of the Fundamentalists, as evidenced by the movie, "Darwin's Dilemma." Recently I was invited to a Presbyterian church where a men's fellowship viewed and discussed this movie. I was put on the spot for my "professional" opinion. There were two points presented in the movie that I felt needed further clarification based on relatively recent scientific findings. They were as follows:

1. Darwin's theory is not substantiated because the great diversity of body shape, as exhibited by the different phyla known as animals, plants, fungi and molds, and unicellular organisms, is not determined by genes. Furthermore no intermediates in these shapes have been observed in all the fossil evidence, again arguing against a slow, "bottom to top" evolution that results from mutations.

2. The enormous diversity in body shape/plan cannot result in such a short time from mutations, even with natural selection as a driving force. Mutations cause very small changes in the structure of proteins, one amino acid at a time, which is not enough to change body shapes significantly, even in billions of years. Therefore, the existing diversity must have resulted from "intelligent design."

The assemblage of body parts is now well known to be controlled by genes, which are comprised of DNA. Drosophila (fruit flies) mutants were found with bizarre assemblages, such as having antennae coming out of their abdomens instead of from their heads, and wings extending out of their heads. The mutations responsible for these abnormalities were located in a gene called hox. Prof. Ed Lewis, a geneticist at CalTech, received a Nobel Prize for this discovery. A gene similar to hox was later found in humans, and once again, mutations in this gene caused abnormalities in body part assembly. When a normal human hox gene was placed into the egg cell of a fly having a mutated hox gene, the egg developed into a normal fly. Thus the human hox gene can cause normal assembly of the body parts even of a fruit fly. This is one of many examples of the similarity in genes present in both humans and lower organisms. The differences in related genes increase gradually as we go down the "evolutionary ladder" from humans to other mammals to birds to plants to molds to amoeba to bacteria, in line with Darwin's theory that all life evolved from a common ancestor.

But how do the very large changes occur, giving rise to the different phyla, and how is it possible to acquire an increase in genetic information? Single cell organisms such as bacteria, E. coli for example, have only a few thousand genes whereas humans have nearly 30,000 genes. Actually we have enough DNA to accommodate far more genetic information than that, but more than 98% of human DNA does not code for proteins. It is not yet known what role most of this so-called "junk DNA" serves, if any. Nevertheless, we lucky humans have 1000 times more DNA than E. coli. Mutations cannot account for how we got it, but the following explanation can.

Experiments have proven that, under certain conditions, all or parts of genes can replicate more than once during a single cell division, thereby giving rise to an increase in genetic material referred to as "gene families." One of the dozens of examples of a gene family includes the genes that code for human hemoglobin proteins. The different types of human hemoglobin include fetal, embryonic and adult, all oxygen transport proteins. The duplicated hemoglobin genes are free to mutate without hurting the organism because the original gene remains intact and functional. The fetal, embryonic, and adult forms of hemoglobin genes actually provide a selective advantage in humans today, functioning as the codes for hemoglobin proteins that are synthesized at different stages of development.

Through recombinations between the duplicated gene and other genes, new genes can be created very rapidly. How do we know this happens, and how fast is this process? Human newborns do not have the genes that code for antibody proteins for nearly six months. During the first six months after departing the womb, genetic recombinations take place in the DNA of B lymphocytes, the cells that produce antibodies. Segments of DNA called exons recombine at random, creating the millions of different genes needed to produce antibodies that can specifically attack the millions of different foreign chemicals ("antigens") that might invade our blood. Thus we know for certain that in the short period of only six months, certain of our cells undergo sufficient DNA recombination to create millions of new genes.

A simple organism such as the Influenza Virus also exhibits genetic recombination quite rapidly. Mutations in the flu virus give rise to the not so serious outbreaks every year, but recombination causes the severe worldwide pandemics that occur approximately every 7 years. Even viruses can undergo genetic recombination when two different viruses, such as swine flu and bird flu, infect the same cell. The resultant recombinant flu viruses are so different from their parents that existing human antibodies fail to recognize them, thus leading to the pandemic.

It is therefore evident that during the nearly four billion years since life first appeared on Earth, a primitive organism could have evolved into the complex life forms present today. This would require not only mutations, but also DNA duplication and recombination in order to create new genes. Both of these genetic processes take place quickly and efficiently. Scientific experimentation has proven the existence of these processes, which together could cause a much more rapid evolution of life forms than that caused by mutations alone. This is not evolution as theorized by Charles Darwin, but not even DNA was known in his time.

It should be noted, however, that none of these findings have any bearing on the question of how the first life form came into existence. Nor do they prove that diverse life forms such as bacteria, fungi, plants, and animals, actually evolved from a common ancestor by the mechanisms described. No scientific evidence can ever **disprove** the existence of a God/Creator, or of life forms that evolve according to His/Her plan, even if scientists one day create a living thing in the test tube and cause it to evolve into a dinosaur. Science is based on experimental evidence; religion is based on faith. It should be possible for them to co-exist in peace and harmony.

ACKNOWLEDGMENTS

I am very grateful to my wife, Lynn, and my son, Sascha (aka Alexander) for their thorough, constructively critical reviews and constant encouragement. Dr. Jack Fisher was the first to insist that these stories be published as a book, and Henry DeVries was instrumental in making this happen. I am indebted to the many people of all ages who read these stories and amazed and encouraged me with their praises.

Most of all I want to thank my thousands of students, and especially my "gang of four" (Sascha, Ari, Danny, and Jessica), who made my career as an educator such an enormous joy. I wish I had the patience and memory to write about each and every one of them.

Made in the USA
Lexington, KY
18 April 2013